The Mayflower Club

A Fictional Novel About a True
Washington, DC, Speakeasy

Sharon Marshall

This is a work of FICTION. The characters, places,
and events in this book are fictitious or are used
fictitiously.

ISBN-13: 978-1547271696

ISBN-10: 1547271698

Author's Note: The Era of Prohibition in the

United States

On a brisk October day in 1929, investors, fueled by a slowing in consumer spending and subsequent stockpiling of raw goods, started dumping stocks. As a bleak day settled into a dark night, twelve million shares of stock were traded. In the coming days, "Black Thursday" prompted panicked investors to continue selling stocks, resulting in banks being unable to sustain the relentless drain of cash. Banks closed, businesses shut down, bread lines formed.

Even before this happened, what was dubbed as the Grand Experiment, Prohibition, had exacerbated the social ills it was supposed to suppress. The Women's Christian Temperance Union (WCTU) had been a giant force behind enacting the 18th Amendment that had made the United States "dry." Effective at first, within a few years the Grand Experiment turned sour. In major cities including Washington, DC, illegal speakeasies thrived. Crime increased, poisonous, unregulated bathtub gin killed imbibers, and speakeasies selling illegal alcoholic beverages popped up everywhere. Washington, DC, speakeasies were not on the same grand scale as Chicago and New York. But they flourished just the same, even after the 1929 crash of the stock market.

In the spring of 1933, President Franklin Delano Roosevelt invoked legislation to heal a weakened nation. Key to his attempt to jumpstart the country, FDR launched "The

New Deal," fulfilling a promise he made in his inaugural address. The plan to restructure the banks, build dams, and pay commodity farmers not to farm to decrease surpluses in wheat, corn, and tobacco, also called for repeal of the 18th Amendment, commonly known as Prohibition. Slapping a tax on the widespread use of alcohol would provide a quick influx of cash to a weary government, not to mention address the menacing problem of a growing crime element known as the Mafia.

It was during this tumultuous time in our nation's history that the actual Mayflower Club, located on Connecticut Avenue in Washington, DC, came into being.

Author's Update 2022: The Mayflower Club

Throughout the book, I directly referenced a present day club which was called the "Dirty Martini." I visited the Dirty Martini while writing the book. I am happy to announce that the club changed owners in 2020 and reopened in late 2021 as the "Mayflower Club." Keeping with the spirit of the book, the name will remain the same Dirty Martini. If you find yourself in Washington, DC, the Mayflower Club is located in DuPont Circle and there are references now to the original 1933 speakeasy. I included a picture on the back cover.

Chapter 1

 *Los Angeles, 2015*

Today was a mess. Just plain messy. I looked down at a desk littered with unpaid bills, worthless magazines, and coffee-stained receipts. Dust bunnies were hanging out in groups and tissues of unknown origin lay scattered about. All I wanted to do was hide. Run away. I glanced again at the unpaid-bill stack. A mistake. Now I could literally see my little archeology company shrinking. I could feel it. Years of worry, struggle, and too much ramen seemed meaningless now. I opened the drawer and looked in an empty cavern once stuffed with project files. Now there was just one. One lowly hanging file. Devil's Lair. My great beacon of hope in Australia. I pulled out the file, shuffled through sheets of paper, grabbed a few documents, and stuffed them into my backpack.

I wasn't broke but needed a good-paying project. I fished through the backpack for my airplane ticket, found it, and heard a knock on the door.

"Melinda, there's a man here who'd like a word with you. I asked if he had an appointment. Of course I knew he didn't, but he seems pleasant and rather … insistent."

My assistant, Bev, was my fifth in five years. I think I'm an agreeable boss but must be horrible at hiring assistants. Bev was a bit older than my usual hires but had impeccable references and met my neurosis for being punctual. Her style of dress was provocative for a late thirtysomething, but I chose to ignore that oversight. I paid a higher salary to get Bev. Maybe throwing more money at the problem would help.

"Tell Mister—"

"Mr. Higgins, Mr. Clarence Higgins."

"What do you think? Worth my time to meet this guy? You know how busy my schedule is."

"Oh Mel, please. I know you're looking for a distraction from whatever it is you're doing right now. The guy's all dressed up. I don't think he's from around here."

"All right, I'll be out in a minute." Somehow Bev sees through me and doesn't have a problem sharing it. Not sure if I like that or not.

She shut the door. I could have followed her out to meet this Clarence Higgins, but making people wait made me feel better. I had nothing to do at the moment, but I continued to sit at my desk.

I stared at the picture of my three kids. One in college, and the other two working at the site in Australia. All successful and, by all appearances happy, but none of them needed me. The remaining picture on my desk was of a blissful Steven and me in Barbados. We'd been dating for three years. I was fairly sure he was cheating on me, but I didn't have it in me to get mad or care. I knew it was time to get rid of Steven, but that required a final decision, some sort of action. Even though I struggled with hiring a good assistant, I was more comfortable making business decisions than personal ones. When it came to men, I was a woman who'd had a string of regrettable relationships. I have always hoped that worn-out relationships would somehow dissolve without any effort on my part. This never happened. I've tried all sorts of devious behaviors. Apparently, I'm not devious enough.

As I sat there, thinking about how to deal with this regretful situation, I looked again at my ticket. Not a pretty picture of a satisfying life. After an unproductive ten-minute pity party, I decided it was time to meet Clarence Higgins.

I walked into the reception area and found a distinguished-looking older gentleman wearing a three-piece dark wool suit. An overcoat draped over his arm, and an umbrella, or was it a cane? Definitely a derby-type hat. Few people in Los Angeles dressed like that today, maybe never. I surmised that he must be sweltering in the heat. As he stood, I noticed that he was struggling. Bev noticed too; she offered to help him with his overcoat. Mr. Higgins, with a professional demeanor, declined.

"Mr. Higgins," I said, walked toward him and shook his hand. "My name is Melinda Danbury. It's nice to meet you."

"Hello Mrs. Danbury. It's a pleasure to meet you."

"It's Ms. Danbury, but please call me Mel. What can I do for you?"

"Would it be all right if we spoke in your office? I won't take much of your time."

No matter how politely said, Bev always takes a brush-off statement personally. Of *course* she wanted to hear what Mr. Higgins had to say. I could feel her frowning behind me.

"When is my next appointment, Bev?" I didn't have a next appointment. But after working with me for the past few months, Bev picked up on the "let's cut this short" drill.

"At two o'clock," she said. That was thirty minutes away. Bev might work out after all.

In my office, I asked Mr. Higgins to have a seat. "Now Mr. Higgins, what may I do for you?"

"Please call me Clarence. I will get right to the point." In spite of the distance, I could see drops of sweat on the man's brow. Clarence was either sweating from the suit or from whatever was on his mind. Either way, he looked miserable.

"Clarence, can I take your coat? I know it's quite warm in here. My air conditioner can't seem to keep up with this late summer heat."

"Thank you, no. I'm fine. I'm from Detroit, you see, where the weather is a bit chillier this time of year. I've never been to Los Angeles let alone California. I'm afraid I don't know how to dress for the weather here."

So far, we'd discussed the weather, determined his place of origin, and noted that he was uncomfortable. Time to move this along.

"You were saying, Mister— sorry, Clarence. The reason for your visit to LA?"

"I am looking for someone. And I understand that you are good at locating things."

"Clarence, I'm an archeologist," I explained. "I locate primitive fossils and bones and excavate old ruins and buildings. My experience is not in locating people. Have you considered a private detective agency? I can provide excellent references in that area."

"Let me explain a bit further." Clarence leaned forward, causing some of the sweat droplets to slide into wooly salt-and-pepper eyebrows. "The man I'm looking for is dead. Been dead for a *long* time. I need to find him, and I also need someone with experience in buried things. And by buried things, let me specify. I'm looking for a large amount of money and I think the dead guy knows where it is."

Looking for a dead guy and money. And the dead guy knows where it is? None of this made any sense, but I did have a slight uptick in interest. Yet, I continued to argue my lack of experience for this kind of request, no matter how intriguing.

"Well. That's certainly interesting, but, Clarence, a detective agency is better equipped to—"

"I'm sorry, Miss Mel, I know how that sounds. I could explain it better, but I know your time is limited. I was referred to you by a good friend and he says you're the best at findin' stuff. I can pay you a decent wage and if we find this dead guy and the money, a handsome finder's fee. If you had more time, I could say more, but I can tell you this, my Uncle Edward was mixed up in illegal dealings in the thirties. He said he was looking for a large sum of money. Now Miss Mel, no one believed him, because there weren't a lot of Black folk back then with a lot of money. At least not in our family. All I'm askin' for is an hour or so of your time to give more details. I'll pay you for it, and if you're still not interested ..." Clarence stopped for effect. "You see, Miss Mel, no one believes my story. I'm not a lunatic. I spent many years looking into this and I know the money's out there. If you don't take my case, well I just don't … know … what I'll do." Shaking his head.

Maybe because it sounded so nuts, I believed him. If I didn't have that fake appointment, I might've had Clarence stick around. But if I didn't keep the fake appointment, he'd doubt anything else I ever said.

"Clarence, I'll admit, I'm … interested. I've never been hired to find a deceased individual who was less than say, four hundred years old and wrapped in linen." Clarence didn't warm up to my humor, so I barged forward. "Let's suppose I decide to meet with you again, hear more of the story. Can you give me just a few details about this dead person and why you need to find him?"

"Please don't think I'm rude, Miss Mel, but it would take too long to provide an accurate picture now. You see, there's more to the job than just finding the dead man."

I sat back in my chair and thought a minute, decided it best to act cool, not too interested. I thought distance plus pressing the issue might help squeeze a few more details.

I leaned forward. "Clarence, I'm going to Australia tomorrow to check on one of my sites. I'll be back in two weeks. Maybe just tell me why you came to Los Angeles? Is the person we're looking for here in California?"

"Miss Mel, I can tell you this. I came here just to meet with you. I will stay as long as necessary. I was afraid if I called first, you wouldn't make yourself available to me. I took the chance and made the trip. I've waited this long. Another few weeks won't change anything. As far as where we're going … we'll start in Detroit, but that's not our final destination."

I stifled the exasperated sigh struggling to emerge. "What is our final destination?"

"Washington, DC," he said.

Chapter 2

 Washington, DC, 1933

The two men peered through the empty building's window. Like a calling card from the approaching storm, leaves, papers, and dust swirled around them. They didn't notice the gusty wind or the rain that began to fall but continued looking in the window, transfixed by what this building would one day contain.

Hirsh Rosenburg stared through the glass until persistent raindrops muddled his vision. He took a watch out of his coat pocket and with a discontented look, confirmed the Realtor was late. If the location weren't so desirable, he would have walked away weeks ago. He blindly continued to look at the watch as his impatience grew. Everyone involved in this deal was incompetent.

After years of opening mildly successful speakeasies, he knew his luck was about to change. His previous clubs were insignificant gin joints. Every location had been raided. But nobody came looking for him. Prohibition still controlled the sale and consumption of alcohol, yet smalltime raids were mere annoyances to the Feds. Newspapers continued to cover raids with splashy pictures of Prohibition agents smashing liquor bottles and lengthy articles naming the latest roundup of drunken bar scalawags, but most customers were only slightly inconvenienced and found liquor in almost every other restaurant and joint in town. The sale of liquor had been illegal for thirteen years. It was now more accessible than ever.

Hirsh put the watch back in his pocket and returned to gazing in the window. He took off his hat and briefly ran his hand through thinning gray hair. The rain from his hair was now dripping down his back, and he regretted leaving his rain slicker at home. He put his hat back on, opened his loose-fitting suit jacket, and tried to dry his hands. As the rain continued to pitter-patter on his hat, he returned his thoughts to the challenge at hand. He hoped this would be his last illegal club. The repeated threat of a raid was becoming an annoyance. Before contacting the agent, he'd thought about waiting for Prohibition to end, but there was too much money to be made now from booze and gambling.

"What do ya think?" a familiar voice yelled in Hirsh's ear.

"I think he's late," Hirsh snapped back.

"No, about the buildin'. What do ya think about the buildin'?"

"We're here ain't we?"

That was no answer, yet this was no surprise to Edward either. He'd been with Hirsh for, what was it ... twelve years now? He'd started out sweeping floors, running errands, one of the few blacks with a decent job. Always honest, Hirsh began to trust him with club matters. After a few years, Edward started handling security, throwing out drunks, keeping an eye on the front door. He took on the role of opening and closing the club, and soon Hirsh began to trust Edward with the take. There were specific rules on handling money and Edward always followed them. But as the years rolled by, and his responsibilities grew, he had to be satisfied with the same low-paying wage. Mildly successful clubs lined Hirsh's pockets, yet Edward barely made a respectable living. At first, he was untroubled with the wages, but as time passed, Edward's indifference gradually transformed from blind obedience to festering resentment.

Hirsh had a temper as nasty as a rattlesnake. Edward wanted to quit more times than he could remember. Yet through all their illegal dealings, Edward never worried about going to jail. There'd been close calls, but somehow Hirsh stayed one step ahead of the Feds. Hirsh always paid the bribe, always knew a way out. Most of their business dealings were shady, a few not so shady. The Mayflower Club would be shady, but Edward had nowhere else to go, no one else to rely on. Shady or not, he planned to stay.

"Well boss, don't know 'bout your realtor, but seems to me, he ain't so good." Edward looked in Hirsh's direction.

"What do you know?" Hirsh barked.

Edward knew plenty.

As they stood there with the rain beating down, Edward noticed a man running toward them holding a briefcase on top of his head, a useless shield from the soaking rain.

"Sorry Mr. Rosenburg. It was the weather. I had—"

"You're late. Get me inside." Hirsh's voice, muffled by the downpour.

"Yes, Mr. Rosenburg, right away."

As they all walked toward the entrance, Hirsh began to take stock of the changes he needed to make. The building's front door was oak and stained a dark brown. Heavy. It would have to go. Not the right entrance for the Mayflower Club. This classy joint would have a black-and-silver double-door entrance. Minor detail, but the Mayflower Club would be full of minor details.

Hirsh wasn't looking to cater to small-time alcoholics looking for a cheap drunk. This club was for senators, millionaires, doctors, lawyers, anyone with clout in Washington, DC. The Mayflower Club had to reflect a sophisticated, classy atmosphere. His clientele would expect nothing less. Hirsh had made regretful mistakes in his previous clubs. Consequently, he was determined to shepherd every detail. Décor, extravagant menu, employees, liquor, and gaming were at the top of the list. He'd leave nothing to chance or to anyone else. Hirsh considered everyone inferior to him. He relied on no one.

The real-estate agent had dreaded this meeting because he always felt nervous around Hirsh. His previous dealings with Hirsh had been confrontational and most unpleasant. With unsteady hands, he fumbled for the keys and as they walked through the door, he leaped into chatter, wanting to spend as little time with the man as possible.

"Now Mr. Rosenburg, you have all four floors. There are stairs to the second floor." A shaky chuckle. "Of course you can see that, they're right in front of you. What am I saying," the last muttered under his breath. A grand mahogany staircase with ornate wooden railing led to a large balcony on the second floor. Guests on the second floor would have a bird's-eye view to the action on the first floor.

"The second floor can be used as an addition to the restaurant, and there are offices down the hall. Around the corner," he pointed to the right side of the restaurant, "there's an elevator that starts on the first floor and stops on the third. You'll need to hire an operator—"

"I got it, I got it. And?"

He continued with his instructions, ignoring Hirsh's unpleasant demeanor. "There are two huge rooms on the third floor, both with two exits that lead to the street. Only you need to know about the third floor. It's not marked on the elevator. That's up to you."

Of course it's up to me, Hirsh thought. *This guy is an idiot.* Most people were idiots, except the rich. They were idiots too, but much easier to tolerate.

"And are you aware of the extra street entrance in the back?" the Realtor asked.

"I am. Any restrictions on what I can build inside?" Hirsh's demeanor softened as he looked around.

"Not to my knowledge." The agent felt more important now. "This is going to be a restaurant, I understand?"

"Ah, yes, a restaurant." Hirsh walked to the left side of the room and gazed up at the wall. "I'd like to build a bar in this space here." Hirsh had turned and spoken to Edward, pointing to the back wall.

This startled the agent. "A bar? You know that booze is still illegal and—"

"Yeah, of course I know. Beer's legal now. We might sell a little of that. But it's only a matter of a few more states.

Booze'll be legal soon enough. I'll be ready when Prohibition ends. In the meantime, I'll be selling food and coffee."

The agent managed to keep his expression neutral, though he didn't believe a word of it. Mr. Rosenburg had no intention of waiting for Prohibition to end. This would be a liquor joint soon enough. But why should that concern him? All he wanted was his share of the commission.

"Construction begins tomorrow," Hirsh instructed to no one in general. He then looked at the Realtor, wanting to move this along. "You got the paperwork?"

"Yes, Mr. Rosenburg. Just one more thing. The owner wants assurance that this will be a proper club," he gathered the documents and reached them out to Hirsh. "He's rather insistent that you sign the liquor documents. You know, the ones stating that no gaming or illegal drinking will occur at the club."

Hirsh was paying almost double the rent. He had no doubt Oscar would be a regular at the Mayflower Club. "Oscar's a weasel. I'll be signing no document. Tell Oscar that I intend to uphold my agreement. As the proprietor of this restaurant, I know my responsibilities. He'll have no trouble. And if there is trouble, he knows where I am."

"Yes sir, I'll relay this to Mr. Benson." The agent busied himself returning the documents to his briefcase, figuring that if the owner wanted to push the matter, he would. He didn't want to get into a heated discussion with a man like Hirsh.

While Hirsh continued to shuffle through the remaining paperwork, Edward began to walk around the club, wondering if his boss understood the work involved to get the place ready. Three floors of construction had to be completed, not to mention ordering and installing the gaming equipment, securing a reliable source for the alcohol, and ordering food for the restaurant. Any opening in less than three months seemed impossible.

The cleanup alone would take at least a couple of weeks. It was obvious that the previous tenants left in a hurry. Dust, broken furniture, even old dishes lay scattered about. Cobwebs were everywhere, and the wood floor was splintered beneath his feet. Every piece of furniture looked unusable. God knew what the other three floors looked like. The list seemed endless.

He walked back toward Hirsh and the Realtor, who was saying, "I'll let Mr. Benson know that you refused to sign the liquor papers. Everything else looks to be in order." The agent shuffled through the documents one last time to make sure he hadn't forgotten any important details. Then, satisfied that his work was complete, he closed his briefcase and as he headed for the door, he stopped, turned around, and looked in Hirsh's direction.

"One last detail, Mr. Rosenburg. When do you plan to open the, ah, restaurant?"

"The Mayflower Club opens in sixty days," Hirsh said as he ambled to where the agent stood and opened the door. "Not a day later."

The Realtor stood too far from Edward to see his widened eyes, but simply nodded and handed Hirsh the keys. With a tip of his hat, he wished Hirsh a good day and gladly escaped into the pouring rain.

Edward couldn't believe what he just heard. Sixty days? Neither he nor Hirsh had experience opening a club with this visibility. Their previous clubs were small joints, mostly hole-in-the-wall style joints located in the seediest parts of town. The Mayflower Club was in the heart of Washington, DC, on Connecticut Avenue. Upscale customers were guaranteed. But so were ill-timed pop-ins from the Feds. And if the booze wasn't enough of a concern, there was the gaming. The stakes for the Mayflower Club couldn't be higher, and now Hirsh expected to open in such an impossibly short time?

Edward didn't know whether to worry about getting caught, or, more productively, devise a plan to make sure he didn't walk away from the club with just his meager salary. As he mulled over these two possibilities, he decided there was no sense in getting too worked up now. The Mayflower Club would open in sixty days, sooner if possible. Hirsh would see to it. It was going to be a relentless rendition of hell for the next few weeks. But in time, Edward hoped his hard work and, doing a bit of scheming, would finally make him a rich man.

After the agent left, Hirsh stood staring at the wall. For the first time, Edward saw a grin on Hirsh's face.

"As I said, the bar is goin' here." Hirsh bent over and spread out his arms as though he was touching the bar. Pointing up toward the wall, he said, "You see the size of that wall? I want a mirror, a big mirror, with 'The Mayflower Club' inscribed on it. And a lady, a beautiful lady that stares at everyone as they walk into the bar. I want that mirror hanging right here, above the bar. It'll be the envy of every liquor joint in DC." He continued to look at the wall as if the mirror were already in place.

"Okay, boss. A mirror. A big mirror. Right away."

Right away. Edward had no idea how he would pull this off. What was he thinking, agreeing to right away? He knew he could find cheap labor. The Depression's merciless grip on the country would see to that. But the mirror? He had no idea where to begin.

Hirsh fixed Edward with a knowing glare. "I've got George to help us get the club ready. If my sorry son-in-law knows what's good for him, he'll work double-time. We'll be hiring the right kind of people, once we're near opening. The construction crew will start on the main floor tomorrow. You and I will be overseein' the details on the third floor. I have a special crew for that. Make a list of what we need. I want that list by tomorrow."

"Yes, boss." Sometimes the fewer words with Hirsh, the better.

Edward took out a notepad and pencil from his rain-soaked satchel, dragged a chair to one of the broken tables, and sat. He watched Hirsh wander around the room, peering up at the ceiling from time to time, scowling at the cobwebs. He opened the notepad and began scribbling words on a sheet of paper. He paused for a minute, looked toward the ceiling, and tried to imagine the all-important money floor. He continued to write, adding tables, chairs, carpeting, a bar, and paneling to his growing, seemingly endless list. This was the fourth joint they'd opened together. The other three joints were successful but had to shut down in a hurry. Sitting there, his mind wandered back to money. Edward had saved a little cash from the last two clubs, but not enough. If this one hit it off with the locals, if he could make it until the end of Prohibition, he'd hoped he could retire from this line of work. But not with the wages Hirsh paid.

There had to be a way to make more money. He'd never betrayed Hirsh's trust, but as he looked up and glanced around the restaurant, he knew this was his last chance to hit it big. He'd been a sucker in the past. Not this time. He felt his head begin to pound. No use in dwelling on the money now; he had a list to make.

He watched Hirsh meander back toward the bar area and remembered the mirror. "Boss, remind me about that mirror. You want the name of the club and a lady on it?"

"Go find an artist," Hirsh said. "There has to be hundreds of outta-work artists in this city. Bring one here and I'll work it out with him. All I need you to do is find a source for the mirror. Can you do that?"

"Yes, boss."

"And on Monday, I need you to go to Spades and meet with Sammy. I told him I need two roulette tables, four, maybe five blackjack tables, card tables. And oh, a few craps tables. Don't forget to bring up the cards, chips, and any other shit I need," Hirsh rambled on. "And tell him I need it all within six weeks." He chortled. "That should guarantee seven. He knew I'd be orderin' soon."

Spades. Edward hated that part of town. Over the years, the upper north side of DC, had become notorious for violent crime against Blacks. He'd heard stories. Crime against Blacks didn't often make the papers. The information Edward got came from the streets. Word was, cops "conveniently" avoided that area.

As if Hirsh read Edward's mind he growled, "And don't let whitey give you any trouble. Take the gun, but don't use it. I can't bail you outta that kind of shit, remember that. If you have must use it, run like hell and don't come back."

Hirsh paused speaking, walked over to him, and rested a hand on his shoulder. "Sammy knows you're coming." Another pause. "Look, if you're going to be my right-hand man, I need to count on you for these errands. I can't be worryin' every time I send you somewhere. For God's sake, it'll be fine."

Edward didn't believe Hirsh. Hard to believe any white man. Hirsh had looked out for him in the past. That was no guarantee for the future. Edward was dreading Monday.

Chapter 3

 Los Angeles, 2015

On the drive home I thought about Clarence Higgins. But mostly about his story, which was intriguing, and ... somehow tinged with an element of danger. I wasn't sure why I felt that way. Everyone involved must be dead by now. Besides, trying to locate a dead man holding clues to a stash of money? That just sounded farfetched. No other way to say it. Maybe when I was younger, I'd have jumped at an offer like that, just for fun. But now? I needed the money, yet the odds of actually getting paid seemed remote. Clarence had appeared sincere, and desperate. But did I want to get involved in this caper?

I pulled into my garage and absentmindedly walked from my car to the elevator. Pushing the button for the fifteenth floor, my thoughts turned to Steven. This day was not getting any better. Wincing, I closed my eyes until the elevator dinged.

I opened the door to my apartment and noticed my daughter sitting on the sofa with a stranger, a stranger who sprang to his feet upon seeing me.

"I'm home," I announced with a pasted-on smile, in case there were any shenanigans going on.

"Yes Mom, I can actually see you," Abby noted, and returned a smile just like mine.

A tall young man in respectable dark blue button-down shirt and ironed khaki pants walked toward me. "Hello Ms. Danbury, I'm Allen," he said as he held out his hand.

Short haircut. Nicely dressed. Not the usual type Abby dated. Not one visible tattoo or a nose ring. Wow, two interesting introductions in one day. "Nice to meet you, Allen." I shook his hand and looked toward my daughter.

Allen spoke first. "Abby and I are working on a physics problem that's due tomorrow. She's a lot better at this stuff than I am."

"She didn't inherit her math skills from me," I admitted.

A familiar, tortured sigh from the couch. "That's a subtle compliment designed to throw my dreams of teaching out the window, all to become an accountant in the family business."

I ignored the comment only because it might be true. As I made my way to the kitchen for a much-needed glass of anything with alcohol I said to Abby, "Sweetheart, I hope you remembered that I leave tomorrow. I'm counting on you to take care of Poodles while I'm gone."

I heard Allen ask Abby, "You have a poodle?"

"We have a German shepherd named Poodles. Mom's idea. There's not a lot of convention in my life." Abby gave an exaggerated shake of her head.

"I heard that," I said, closing the shutters between the kitchen and living room. But I couldn't resist eavesdropping through the tiny open slats while I poured a glass of wine.

I saw Allen look toward Abby. "My parents are traditional. Kinda conventional. Mostly boring. I like your mom's attitude. Believe it or not, Abby, you take after her."

"Did you hear that Mom?" Another dart hurled my way. I ignored that too.

Glass in one hand, three sets of silverware in the other, I emerged from the kitchen to set the table.

"Where are you traveling to?" Allen looked my way.

"Australia."

"Never been there. Vacation?"

"Nope. Work. In the world of archeology, Australia's a goldmine. I've been more times than I care to think about, and not once for vacation. We're excavating a site called Devil's Lair. I have a small team on-site. Every now and then I need to check on them. They hate it when I show up, and that's why I love to go."

"My mom's also a masochist." Accompanied by an extra-dramatic eye roll.

"Now Abby, you're being a bit dramatic. As much as I'm sure you both would like me to stick around, I need to start packing. Staying for dinner, Allen?"

"Thank you. No. Heading out shortly, in fact."

"Well you're certainly invited. Hope we see you again. Good luck with physics."

* * *

In the bedroom, I grabbed the first suitcase I could find. Looking in my closet, I grabbed a cobalt blue gabardine suit, threw a multicolored scarf around my neck, and walked over to the mirror. I unclipped my black hair and let it fall to my shoulders. The suit matched the color of my eyes and the red earrings I was wearing picked up the deep red in the scarf. Not bad. I rifled through my closet, grabbed a few more suits, in case I had any business meetings, and finished with rough-and-ready clothes for the jobsite. Years of packing, and I'm still lousy at it. Even knowing that it would be a short stay, I stuck to my usual tendency to over pack, giving little thought to what I threw in the suitcase. One advantage to not wasting time thinking: I was literally done in less than ten minutes.

I heard the front door close—Allen leaving. I meandered back to the kitchen to throw dinner together. My cooking was better than my packing. I find cooking enjoyable. Fresh vegetables tossed into a hot wok and some of last night's chicken, a dash of this and a pinch of that, done.

I looked up as Abby walked into the kitchen. Pouring a second glass of white wine I said, "I hope you're staying for dinner. I'd like to talk to you." Young she might be, but my daughter has the insight ability of someone twice her age.

"Well lucky for you, I don't have to be at the restaurant until eight thirty," she said. "And I must say, whatever you're cooking smells good."

We filled our plates, took our places, and I briefed her on my interesting visit from Clarence Higgins.

"Dig up a dead guy? Really Mom, I know you dig up dead stuff for a living, but usually it involves wings or scary-looking teeth, or something related to clay."

"I tried to talk him out of hiring me, but he insisted. Said I was recommended by someone. He wouldn't say who. Anyway, I don't have many details. He also mentioned a stash of money."

She stopped chewing. "Where is this … this dead guy? And how much money?"

"I'm not sure about either. Detroit or in DC, I think. Maybe neither. As for the money, I'm not sure he even knows."

She went back to chewing, her forehead wrinkled. "That's rather vague. Didn't he share anything else?"

"Well that's my fault. I pulled the fake-appointment routine in case the guy was insane. Still not sure he isn't. But my fake appointment prevented a complete explanation."

"The scam always backfires."

"I know. It seems like such a good idea at the time, too. Anyway, I couldn't change the trip to Australia, and I'm meeting with him when I get back. Have to admit, I am somewhat curious. He also mentioned other buried things he wanted me to find."

"The plot thickens. Maybe you need to let Steven know."

A subject I was hoping to not discuss tonight, but she started it. "There's my next problem. I'm dumping Steven when I get back. I'd do it now, but that'd be too easy. I'd rather worry about it during my trip, put too much pressure on myself, and then dump him in a panic when I get back." Abby stared at her dinner and without comment, shook her head.

"In any case," I continued, "I doubt Steven would be helpful. Although I guess he means well, his advice never helps. And even if it did, I'm … bored lately. And I just recently figured out he's part of that."

Still no response. I'd have to spill everything. A deep breath, and I dove in. "And in an ironic twist, I think he finds other women more interesting than me. I don't have proof, but I don't need it. It might just be my excuse to justify dumping him." No comment from Abby. Time to move on. "But enough about my pathetic relationship, what's the story with the polite physics guy?"

"I'm not sure yet." Eyes still on her plate. "Nice enough. But almost too nice. And he's right about his parents. They're dull as dirt."

"The apple doesn't fall far from the tree you know," I advised as I picked up my glass.

"If only those old sayings were true…" Abby looked at me with a doubtful expression.

"You're too young to understand, but the old sayings usually do hold up."

"Note taken."

I gave her a list of what to take care of while I was away. Abby has many attributes and thankfully reliability is one of them. She complains but doesn't let me down.

After we finished dinner, I tidied up the kitchen and walked back to the bedroom to add some last-minute items to the suitcase. I was agonizing over where to shove them in when I heard the phone ring. Steven. I decided to let him roll over to voicemail. I'd call back as I boarded my flight. As I closed the suitcase, I mulled over the fact that I'd had two new, interesting introductions in one day. Don't those things run in threes? Or maybe that's deaths, or lottery winnings. As I pondered over what new and interesting person I might meet next, I checked to make sure I had my passport and other travel docs. The flight to Perth had never been interesting, and I'd booked my usual stale hotel full of overly excited tourists. Certainly no chance there. But I could hope. And get some sleep to prepare for a long day tomorrow.

* * *

Sometimes it doesn't work out well, but this Saturday, the car service was right on time. I kissed Abby goodbye, gave Poodles a pat on the head, and ran out the door. Over my shoulder I shouted, "I fed her already, but take her for a walk before you head to school." I heard a muffled reply I hoped was a yes.

Keeping my vow of last night, I called Steven and thankfully got his voicemail. I said something about calling soon. No words of affection or "I'll miss you." Pathetic.

I made it through the airport just in time to board the flight. As I settled into my seat, I noticed an attractive couple sitting in the row across the aisle. I had what appeared to be a ninety-year-old man sitting next to me. He was dressed in khaki pants, a crisp light blue shirt and had a Panama type hat placed on his lap. He had rosy cheeks and perfectly groomed light gray hair. With Steven and the stress of my finances on my mind, I wasn't in the mood for cheery conversation. Maybe he was hard of hearing, or the silent type. The latter would be good. The couple glanced my way and then went back to their conversation. Excellent. After take-off, I grabbed my iPad and headphones, just in case the old guy had an idea about making conversation. It's a long flight to Perth and I had my sights on watching old movies and catching up on a few books. Hopefully the guy would make it all the way. I didn't want him dying in the seat next to me.

A brief stopover in Sydney, and we landed in Perth. Thankfully, my seat companion still lived. The attractive couple gathered their belongings and exited the plane. I lingered a few minutes and waited politely for my rosy-cheeked friend to gather his suitcase and belongings. With a happy grin and a tip of his hat, he wished me a good day. My ability to misread people was becoming an epic personality flaw. I was spending too much time with inanimate objects. Maybe that's why I picked archeology. Either way, it was time to be a better person and start caring about humanity. It's what people did. I'd start that at some point.

It was shortly after six p.m. when we landed. Too late to go to the jobsite. Devil's Lair was a three-hour drive, which I would tackle tomorrow. I thought about calling the kids or getting a Poodles check-in with Abby, but changed my mind. After checking into the hotel, I needed a few drinks to unwind and decided to head back down to the bar.

As I walked into the restaurant, I noticed the attractive couple from the flight at a table near the entrance. I sat at the bar, ordered a stiff drink, and to my surprise they both rose from the table and walked toward me.

"Weren't you on our flight from Los Angeles?" the woman said with an Australian accent.

"Yes I believe I was."

She gave me a beaming smile. "I'm Bette, like Bette Midler, only my last name is Wellford, and this is my brother, Jaimie. You're from America?"

Brother? I'd assumed they were a couple. But then my assumptions were usually more miss than hit. My memory of late, too, but hearing the man's name, a faint connection clicked. Just not hard enough.

"Jaimie Wellford? It seems I've heard that name before." Spoken as I looked his way. It wasn't a pickup line; it was actually true. "And yes I am ... from America."

"Well Jaimie here runs the Wangara Production Company. Maybe that's why you've heard his name. We were in LA trying to convince Warner Brothers to work with us on their next picture. Not looking good for us, but who needs them."

"I guess I should speak for myself," Jaimie said in a heavy Australian accent. "And Warner Brothers gave us a bit of a knock back, but they'll see it my way."

Short, dark, wavy hair, tanned complexion, and piercing green eyes. He reached out to shake my hand. I somehow stuttered out, "Melinda. Melinda Danbury. But please call me Mel."

"Right, Melinda, what brings you to Perth?" Jaimie said.

Still trying to compose a thought, any thought, I rambled, "I run a small archeology company and one of our sites is here. Devil's Lair. Maybe you've heard of it?" I had to throw a question back their way to give me a moment.

Bette's face brightened even more. "Yes I have. I've been there several times. Mostly for filming, but it's a fascinating place. Various archeology companies have been digging around on that site for years. I didn't realize there was still work going on."

"Probably busier than ever," I asserted. "I have ten or so employees and grad students working there now."

"That doesn't sound like a small company," Jaimie said. "Is that your only site?"

"At the moment, yes," I confirmed with slight embarrassment. "I'm scouting a few additional locations, but right now my focus is Devil's Lair." This was mostly true. "Do you both live here?"

"Yes we do," Jaimie answered. Uh oh. I'd begun to wonder if this guy was married. "We grew up here. My dad was in the film business, and I took the company over after he retired. Bette's in charge of our production facilities, and our youngest sister is the HR manager." He smiled. "We don't believe in nepotism, but we just happen to have shit-hot family."

Shit-hot family. Must be an Australian phrase. Though technically it had been more than twenty-four hours, I counted this as the third interesting introduction of the day.

Jaimie looked over my shoulder as if he'd spotted someone he knew. "Charley's here, Bette. Do you want to join us?"

"No." Bette shook her head. "You're on your own. I'm too tired."

"Well then ladies, excuse me." Jaimie touched my arm as he made this declaration.

"Of course." I looked directly in his eyes, trying to make a lasting impression.

"Hope to run into you again, then." Jaimie winked in my direction. Or was there something in his eye?

As he walked away, I said to Bette, "We just flew twenty hours and your brother has a meeting? I can barely put a coherent sentence together I'm so tired."

Laughing, she lowered herself onto the barstool next to me. "He works twenty-four hours a day. I don't have that drive. I have kids and a husband that expect me to show up at home. Jaimie doesn't. I'm content to let him run the show. Speaking of which, I told Jaimie I would wait until Charley showed up. He's here now, so I really should shove off. I'd like to visit Devil's Lair. It's been years since I have seen the place."

Well, that answered the marriage question.

I reached into my purse and handed her my card. "Call anytime. Two of my children are working at Devil's Lair. They feel they must entertain me, so I'm sure they'll be happy if I have a diversion."

"Great. I'll give you a call. Glad we ran into you. I don't know if you noticed, but Jaimie kept looking at you on the flight. He can be annoying. He would've said hello, but he thought you weren't interested in conversation."

"I was more concerned about the guy next to me wanting to chat the whole flight," I said, embarrassed by the confession.

"You might just hear from him."

I wasn't sure what to say to this. "I think I'll walk out with you, Bette."

Bette walked over to her brother to say goodbye, and as I met her to leave, I felt two sets of eyes following me on the way to the exit.

Chapter 4

 *Washington, DC, 1933*

In just a few short days, work was well underway to convert the old building into the Mayflower Club. The antiquated front door had been replaced with black double doors edged in silver trim. Gleaming silver door handles were being installed and red velvet ropes, which led up to the entrance, were being attached to matching silver poles. A marquee with "The Mayflower Club" emblazoned on it led to the front door. The entrance's floor, parquet stone colored black and deep gray, was half completed. Mixed in the stone were tiny specks of gold that glistened in the sunlight filtering through the tall windows.

Inside the club, workers were busy hammering, sanding, sawing, and assembling. Edward had no idea where Hirsh found all these workers. But then he didn't know all of Hirsh's secrets, and there was no purpose in asking. Nor did

Edward care. The sooner the club opened, the sooner he could make money.

The mirror had turned into a frustration. Edward hadn't yet found a source. A solid mirror, no less than eight feet tall and six feet wide, was hard enough to find. To have it etched with the name of the club and a picture of a woman increased the difficulty. There were many details, yet this one task consumed him. He'd done an exhaustive town-wide search, and had no luck finding a mirror that big, let alone an artist.

And then there was Hirsh's son-in-law, George. For the past eight years, Hirsh dragged that no-account George along to every club he opened. Hirsh's daughter, Cecilia, was a drunk and worthless as a mother. Hirsh knew his daughter was a lush, but, from worry or pride, or maybe both, he never discussed it with anyone. Yet everyone knew. Cecilia was his only child. Hirsh confided to Edward that he regretted the marriage to his "lunatic" first wife and if he was honest, he regretted his daughter too. Edward thought this was a sorrowful confession. He'd never settled down with a family and was uncomfortable commenting on the situation. He did understand the burden Hirsh undertook to make sure his granddaughter, Dottie, was financially taken care of. The employment of George took care of that.

But making sure Dottie didn't go without presented a sizable problem for Edward. George treated him like a second-class citizen. Less than second class. And no matter how Hirsh tried to pretend his son-in-law was a decent fellow, Edward was hard pressed to believe George was any better a father than Cecelia was a mother. Lazy, disheveled, George was a louse of a man who never put in a day's work as long as Edward had known him. Edward had heard vague stories about abuse too. Since George was related to Hirsh, there would be no complaining. While he felt empathy toward Dottie, getting involved was useless, so he simply decided to stay clear of white people's business.

Hirsh had instructed George to oversee construction on the first two floors. They'd gutted the first floor over the weekend and George's so-called job was to make sure the workers stayed busy, that construction plans were followed and that he ordered a list of required materials. Edward was ultimately responsible for all three floors but was glad his focus was the third floor. This included all the food, liquor, and gaming setups. He had no idea what George was being paid, but assuredly knew it was more than Hirsh paid him. He winced to think how much more. Didn't seem fair, but as Edward saw it, Jim Crow meant nothing was fair for blacks. He knew he had it better than most, but the disparity stuck in his craw.

At last, George ambled in for the day. Hirsh ignored George as he often tried to do and spotted Edward. "How's the mirror comin'?"

"I think I have a source," Edward lied, "but the etching is complicated. That's gonna cost us big."

"It don't matter. All I care about is delivery. Not openin' without it. Six weeks. You have five. Less I'm hoping."

"Do you need help?" George chimed in.

Hirsh snapped back, "You have plenty to do. No need gettin' sidetracked. Edward can handle this. I've got chairs and tables showing up and I need the floor finished. Focus on that, will ya?"

"Got it, Hirsh. I'll have everything ready in time." He looked right at Edward as he smugly replied.

Hirsh scowled at Edward. "Heading upstairs for a few minutes. Keep an eye on things."

"Yes boss."

* * *

Hirsh took the stairs to the second floor and walked to his corner office. He sat at his desk and as he leaned back in his chair, he pondered over his liquor supplier options. Liquor was easier to get now, but with the scuttlebutt about the laws easing soon, bribes were more expensive. The risk of Prohibition agents working inside liquor and gaming distributors was at an all-time high. His last raid came at the hands of an informer who'd wormed his way inside his longtime booze supplier's operation. Expensive lesson to learn. Hirsh hashed over all the available suppliers in the DC, area. Though he rarely did anymore, he prayed to the Lord Almighty for a wise choice. His old sources had literally dried up, and his contacts in DC, were limited. Taking the advice of other club owners was risky. No one wanted successful competition. All Hirsh could count on was bribing anyone and everyone. It would cost a fortune, but his vision, and the profit the Mayflower Club would bring, was worth it.

Hirsh ran his little organization with a pecking order in mind. He handled security and staff hiring, and ordered all gaming equipment and booze, leaning on the lists Edward and George supplied. He relied on Edward to oversee construction, including construction workers, and he'd manage the bar and waitstaff after the club opened. He trusted Edward to stock the bar too—well, once they began serving liquor—and to collect all the cash from the games and booze at the end of each night. It took years for Hirsh to trust Edward, but little by little, and with a wary eye, he'd added these tasks to Edward's daily schedule.

Hirsh walked out of his office and leaned over the railing. Looking down to the first floor, he found Edward and with a sweeping arm, motioned him to come upstairs.

"Yes boss?" Edward said, breathing heavy from the walk upstairs.

Once inside, Hirsh closed the door. "Edward, there's something about George lately. Have you noticed him acting… peculiar?"

Edward took a moment to think about this. Of course he noticed George's erratic behavior. But it was no different in the last few years. He decided to play this one low and safe. "I don't know what you mean, boss, he seems the same to me."

Hirsh leaned back in his chair and folded his hands on top of his belly. "Come on Edward, we both know he's a lazy SOB but it seems to me he's worse lately."

Still playing it safe, Edward didn't respond.

"Keep an eye on him, would ya? This club ain't the same as the others. I can't have him screwin' things up here. And I can't fire him. Best if you watched him for me."

Somehow he'd known this was coming. "Yes boss."

"And if you see anything I need to know about, tell me, cause now it's your neck on the line for this." He leaned forward in the chair and pointed at Edward. "Don't fuck this up."

"I'll tell ya, boss," Edward replied and was pretty sure he'd buried the dejection he felt.

"Okay. Glad we understand each other. Now get back to work."

* * *

After Edward closed the door, Hirsh drew out his watch from his coat pocket. The gold chain had broken years ago, but having it repaired seemed not right somehow, as though doing so would alter his memory of the person who gifted it to him. His brother had given him the watch when he knew he was dying. Maybe someday he'd get it fixed.

A click opened the watch, and a glance at the clock face made him wince. He had to stop at home and then head to the liquor distributor. Just enough time for both. He grabbed his hat, ran down the stairs, and as he was about to exit the club, he saw a low-down son of a bitch standing by the bar.

"Oscar, my friend, glad you stopped by." Hirsh forced a grin.

Oscar chose to ignore Hirsh. He walked to the back of the restaurant, looked around the club, and then headed in Hirsh's direction. Hirsh couldn't help but notice that Oscar's three-piece suit was a tight fit. Or that his belly protruded out of the undersized jacket. The man had perennial sweat on his forehead and his hands were always greasy. Hirsh shuddered to think what caused this affliction.

After a moment or two Oscar proclaimed, "Looks like construction is well underway here. I understand from the Realtor that you will open in less than what, a few months from now? That seems optimistic."

"Look around you." Hirsh motioned with both hands in the air. "Work goes on twenty-four hours a day, for which I am paying a fuckin' fortune."

"I can imagine. But I assure you I'm not concerned with your problems, Hirsh. The Realtor says you won't sign the liquor papers."

Hirsh put his arm around Oscar's saggy shoulders and led him to a corner of the restaurant. "Look Oscar, you didn't let me take this place thinkin' I was just cookin' goddamn steaks. I'm paying a hell of a lot of money for this place, and you know it. Everything's covered. And if not, I take the heat."

"What's my guarantee you take the heat? I need some sort of financial guarantee."

"That's bullshit, Oscar. We had a square deal. I know what you're askin'. You want a cut, like every other bloodsuckin' thief in this business."

Oscar shook his head. "Getting worked up ain't gonna change the situation."

Hirsh was not in the mood for this. "Goddammit, Oscar, I thought the higher rent covered all this."

"It doesn't. Five percent more, including booze and cards."

"That was never part of the deal."

Oscar just looked at Hirsh for second or two, and then tapped his finger on his chin. "Only problem is, how can I prove I'm getting my five percent?"

"You can't. We both know that. It's not like I'm keepin' records here."

Hirsh didn't want to give another five percent of his profits away but could see that Oscar wasn't budging. He decided he'd figure a way out of this at some point but now wasn't the time. Hirsh thought for a moment and looked in Edward's direction.

"Edward, come here."

Edward didn't like Oscar at all. Slimy fat old man.

"Oscar, my partner Edward. He'll make sure you get the numbers."

Oscar looked Edward up and down. "I ain't trusting this man. You get me someone else," he said, almost as a commandment.

"His word's as good as mine. You have a problem, you see me. Edward will get you the numbers twice a month. I don't have time to handle that myself. You let me take this place because you know I'll pay the rent, without a problem and at almost double the askin'. Booze'll be legal soon. Even if it ain't, the place'll be full of filthy-rich DC, bigwigs, bringing in their whores, spending money boozing and playing the numbers. And since most of them work for the government, no one is taking us down and you know it."

Oscar didn't know it. Hirsh had one of the best reputations in the illegal booze business, yet it was still illegal. But what did he really care? As long as he got a piece of the action and it couldn't trace back to him, he was in. All he was, was the landlord. Seemed simple to him.

"I want another runner," Oscar demanded once again.

Hirsh didn't want to lose this club. He knew Oscar's word meant nothing and the slightest provocation might undercut this deal, but he also knew that if he didn't stand up to him now, Oscar would have the upper hand. Hirsh had no choice but to stand firm. "You ain't getting it. Edward here, he's the only one I trust. It's Edward or nothing. I ain't got time for horseshit, Oscar." Ignoring any response from Oscar, Hirsh looked at Edward. "On every other Tuesday, give Oscar his *dividends*."

"Yes, boss. Every other Tuesday," Edward repeated, and risked looking at Oscar with open disdain.

"Do you even know what every other Tuesday means?" Oscar asked with contempt for Edward.

"Yes I do, suh."

"Enough of this," Hirsh bellowed and glared Oscar's way. "I've got a meeting to get to. You got what you came here for. I'm telling you how it'll work." Hirsh started to walk toward the door.

"Just one more thing," Oscar followed Hirsh and tugged on his arm to stop him. "If I were to show up one evening with a fine young lady, where exactly would I want to go?"

Hirsh took a moment to calm down. "Let's just say the fine young lady is thirsty. Maybe she would like some … coffee. I would take her to the third floor. And if this young lady would like entertainment, the back room might have what she's looking for. Not easy to get to, but since you own the place, I'm sure you'll know where it is."

"Indeed I do. Just make sure to stay out of trouble, Hirsh. I understand the situation here, but I do not want scandal on my property. Your reputation is good. I did my research. But that don't mean I ain't concerned."

"I can assure you,' Hirsh stated with confidence, "I ain't lookin' for trouble neither."

"I'll be keeping an eye on my investment, Hirsh. Please do not underestimate me. It would not be wise for your health. And please do not cheat me out of what is rightfully mine," he shifted his gaze to Edward.

"Don't threaten me, Oscar." Hirsh leaned into him with his finger tapping on Oscar's chest. "I'm about to make us all rich. I don't need your fucked-up threats. Jesus H. Christ

…" He put his hand on his head and tried to calm down. "Look, it's your property. Come by whenever you want. But don't threaten me or anyone else here."

"Just remember what I said." Oscar's gaze on Hirsh was direct, unwavering. Not waiting for a reply, Oscar walked toward the front door, turned around, looked at them both, opened the door, and left.

"I hope he won't be no trouble, boss," Edward said.

"Well I hope I didn't make a mistake dealin' with that moron. I will *not* let that man take us down, Edward."

"I know, boss," Edward said, and believed it.

Edward walked toward the bar area, bolstered by the thought that it wouldn't be long before the Mayflower Club was a booze-guzzling, card-playing money machine. He knew he had to come up with a plan to siphon money out of the club, or he'd be as broke as he was now. But he was haunted by the same uneasy feeling he had when they opened previous clubs. Not to mention the stakes were higher and the risks too. Hirsh had kept him out of trouble so far, but that was when bribing the Feds was easier. These were different times. All Edward could hope was that booze became legal, quick. He wasn't necessarily worried about the gaming. That was well hidden. Maybe he should worry about that too, but decided now wasn't the time.

"I've got a few errands to run," Hirsh said to Edward. "Get over to Sammy's and take care of that list."

"Yes, boss."

Edward walked to the front of the restaurant and took the elevator to the third floor. The elevator was well hidden behind a wall that opened only when tapped in a certain spot, and the wall was behind two partitions. Hard to find if the club were raided, and most customers would never know it existed. This was for employees, and only the best customers as a convenient exit. Edward took the time to know every entrance and exit in the joint. In a raid, it was every man for himself. That included the ladies. Chivalry didn't exist in a raid.

Edward exited the elevator on the third floor. Construction had just begun there. He walked over to two men handily tearing apart the old bar. They glanced his way but decidedly chose not to notice or acknowledge him. Edward was sure that Hirsh would've drawn more respect. He shook his head and then looked around the room. This was the money floor. The décor had to be perfect. A total of eight chandeliers were on order. Dark mahogany wood for the walls and a deep-red carpet with three-inch padding would cover the main floor. To provide a sultry, soft ambiance, subdued lighting fixtures had been ordered to complement the style and the light from the chandeliers. Mahogany bar stools, with thick, velvet-covered padding, would line the ornate, floor-length bar. This floor would dazzle.

Edward walked toward the window. One more detail to consider. He had to cover the windows to prevent anyone from seeing inside. The coverings needn't be blackout shades here on the third floor. Shutters, maybe? As he glanced out the window with a vacant stare, he noticed two men looking at the club. They were talking to each other, and one of them pointed toward the club. Edward backed away from the window, but continued to watch. They didn't look like Feds. But he couldn't be sure. Was he just paranoid now? The building was under construction and maybe the men were curious. He stood and watched for a few minutes. One man took out a notebook and started writing. As he saw the man put the notebook away, he thought he noticed a holster. Edward made a mental note and moved on.

In the gaming room, he measured a few last items and then took the elevator to the second floor. The noise from the hammering was giving him a headache. The swirling dust began to grate on his allergies. As he stood at the top of the stairs, he drew a handkerchief from his pocket and wiped his nose. After a few minutes of taking in the disaster that lay before him, he remembered he had to walk over to Spades. He went back to Hirsh's office and took out a piece of paper from his coat pocket. He stared at the numbers, turned the dial, and opened the safe. Inside, he found the loaded gun and placed it in his coat pocket, closed the safe, and made his way down to the first floor. He exited the club into a bright sunny sky, having forgotten about the two men he'd seen earlier.

As he turned the corner, he felt a tap on his shoulder. "Can we talk to you for a minute?" one of the men asked as he flashed a silver badge.

Chapter 5

Australia, 2015

As I drove to Devil's Lair, my mind slipped to thoughts of Jaimie. I barely met the guy, but there was an attraction there. On both of our parts. I was sure of it. Successful, good-looking, a catch by all standards. But single? Maybe gay? Maybe I was imagining the attraction? Too many maybes. And most likely too many hurdles. Serial killer? Not likely. Another cheater like Steven? Possibly. Thinks too highly of himself? Most likely. Egotist or not, the man was intriguing.

I heard my phone vibrating in my purse and saw my son's name on the screen.

"Hi David, I—"

"Hi Mom. Where are you?"

"About an hour away. How are you and your sister?"

"Well I'm good …"

"Is something wrong with Jane?"

"Nothing per se. I mean she's healthy and all that, but I'll let her tell you when you get here."

"Care to give me a hint?" I continued to probe.

"I'll just say that you will mostly be happy. Maybe slightly mad."

"David, you're talking in circles." I had to move on. "Let's talk about the site for a minute. How's it progressing?"

"Mom, can we talk when you get here? It's busy and I just wanted to see when you'd be here."

I resigned myself that this conversation was going nowhere. "See you in a little bit."

David heard the aggravation in my voice. "Love you, Mom."

Before I could respond, I heard a click.

It had been six weeks since my last visit to Australia. Longer than usual, and I felt as though I'd neglected the project. I stopped at the main gate, flashed my pass, and drove to our company trailer. Truth be told, I still like seeing "Danbury Archeology, LTD" posted on the side of the trailer. I only hoped I could keep the company afloat.

David and Jane were not in the trailer. I stopped at the front desk, said my obligatory hellos to the staff, and wandered back to my office.

"It's been forever since we've seen you, Mel," my slightly over-dramatic assistant Deb said. "You look fabulous!"

"I know. I feel just awful about it, too. Not my looks. At my age I'll take fabulous. I mean about the site. I know you

and William are completely capable. I almost feel unneeded."
I somewhat believed it.

"William does okay, but he's not you. Just know you're missed."

"Thank you. I miss you guys too. Where are my kids?" I had to change the subject. I'm not good with bullshit adoration.

"I called David as soon as I saw you drive up. He's not far away. Jane will be in any minute. She has some recent news to tell you. I won't spoil it."

"David alluded to 'news,'" I said, trying to probe again. "Tell me, will I like this news?"

"Yes! Now just know that I only have the smallest of details. She wanted to wait until you got here."

William, my site manager, walked in. Tall, trim, tan complexion with short, light brown hair and sparkling blue eyes. Early forties, but he had that older distinguished look that only men are blessed with. I think he shopped at the same store as Indiana Jones.

"G'day, Mel. Welcome back."

I gave him a brief handshake and noticed he looked better than ever. Calm, relaxed.

Just then, Jane walked in. She, on the other hand, looked nervous, and I thought I saw tears in her eyes. Deb looked at me, then at Jane and William.

"I'll be going now," Deb said and quickly exited the office.

I gave Jane a big hug and noticed she was shaking.

"What's all this about?" I didn't hide my concern.

"Mom, I'm glad you're here. I need you to sit down. I'm just going to come out and say it. Now don't get mad. I'm happy."

"I won't get mad. What is it?" Now I was getting mad.

"I got married." Jane winced as she said the words. I almost didn't hear her.

"You got what?" I said in a slightly irritated manner.

"More to the point, William and I got married ... to each other."

"You did what? To whom?" I couldn't believe what I'd heard. Not that this was horrible news. But what did she just say?

"Mel, I wanted to tell you before the wedding," William stammered as his relaxed demeanor slipped away. "But it was Jane's decision."

"And, no, Mom, I am not pregnant."

That thought hadn't occurred to me just yet. "You're married? When did this happen?" Realizing the comment sounded like something you'd say at a crime scene, I softened it a bit. "I guess I mean, why so sudden?" I looked up at William. "You know I like you and I'm happy for both of you, but why the rush? Sounds a bit ... impulsive."

Jane laughed through her tears. "This, coming from a mother who's a poster child for impulsive behavior."

"Well, true. But still, I didn't even know you were dating. I was suspicious like everyone else around here but ..."

Nervous, William responded, "Come on Mel. Dating the boss's daughter? I didn't want it to look like I was, well ... dating the boss's daughter. If it makes you feel any better, I love your daughter to pieces." He looked at Jane for effect.

"We both knew what we wanted and a grandiose wedding suited neither of us."

"William, let me take it from here." Jane looked at him, signaling him to leave.

"Jane is better at this than me. I'll leave you two alone, but Mel, believe me, your daughter is in good hands." William smiled. "I'll just let myself out."

* * *

"Okay, Mom. Look, I'm sorry we didn't tell you. We didn't tell anyone. It does look impulsive, but I gave this decision a lot of thought."

"Your brother and Deb knew," I threw out there in a hurt tone, which was beginning to replace mad.

"We got married on Saturday. They only found out this morning. I tried to wait for you before I told anyone, but I just got so excited."

"What did you wear?" I had no idea where that question came from. "Okay, that was stupid. I just always envisioned helping you get dressed on your wedding day. And don't tell me that sounds silly. I know it does."

"No it doesn't, Mom. My intention wasn't to upset you. And I do mean that. But this felt one-hundred-percent right for William and me."

"William lives here. And you're just visiting. Are your plans to live here?" I was hoping for a no.

"For right now, yes. But I'm assuming we'll be traveling to sites, just like you did when you were young. I'm not abandoning my life in the States. My family's important too. But I'm married to William, and our life's here, for now."

I sat down in my chair. I knew what "for now" meant.

"Mom, I'm living with a man I love, who loves archeology, like I do. Okay, he's a bit older than me but I'm beyond happy with my decision and … I hope you'll be too."

I hadn't thought of that either. William must be almost fifteen years older than Jane. More than that, maybe. As far as I knew, William had never been married. I realized I knew nearly nothing about his family or his background, beyond what I learned from his job interview.

"Where's William's family?"

"They live in Sydney. And before you ask, I've only met them twice. His mom, dad, and brother are coming out on Thursday. We thought we'd have a small party on Saturday at our place."

All I heard was blah, blah *our place*. "I see. You're all moved into his place, then?" My voice took on a few extra high tones.

"It's our home, and I'm mostly moved in. Why don't you stay at my old place instead of the hotel?"

"That's a plus," I tried to concede, but came off sarcastic.

If I didn't get hold of myself, I'd risk losing my daughter. I cleared my throat and plucked a rock from my desk, one I used as a paperweight. "Jane … of course I'm happy for you and William. Just a little stunned. My oldest daughter got married. Such a big step. You know that marriage … well, relationships in general … aren't my strong suit." I gave her a weak smile. "I'm fairly sure you're more responsible in that area than I am. As you get older you tend to admit failings, and relationships have always been my Achilles heel. I've made peace with it. Sort of." I paused. "I'm sorry, did you say something about a party?"

"Yes, Mom. This Saturday." She reached out and touched my shoulder as though she were the parent, comforting her confused child.

"Is that something I can help with, or is it already planned too?" I asked, then cursed my condescending tone.

"I might deserve that, but I'll let it go. Please help me with this party. Planning parties is your gig, not mine."

She was right, and the idea cheered me a little. "Well, since my schedule is clear. Look, I'm still not thrilled about the wedding planning, but since I seem to be the only one upset about it, I'll get over it. And I'm happy for you and William. I just don't know much about him. Except for the excellent work he does here."

"Well, I know enough for us both. Thanks, Mom." She hugged me in that daughterly way.

"Does your sister know?"

"I called her this morning. She wishes she could come out for the party. I'll bring her out here later this year."

"Well that covers all the important people."

"What about Steven?" Jane said. "Is he still around?"

My smile was tight. "Hanging on by a thread. He'll be gone when I get back."

"I never really liked him," she admitted. "Nice enough, but not suited for you."

Nothing to counter there. "I know. I've just been too lazy to dump him. I'm sure he won't be heartbroken."

Jane broke the silence. "Are we good, Mom?"

"There's never any question about that," I said and meant it.

"Okay, cause I need to get back to work."

"How's it going here?"

She went to the visitor's chair and lowered herself into it while she answered. "Quality finds? Few and far between. William's good at keeping the staff motivated," there was pride in her voice. "But it's tedious. We've made progress in the Atlantic Section. Have him show you the beads and skeletal remains. We need to put them through carbon."

"The grants run out in 2018. Do you think we have enough discovery to stay here that long?"

"Oh my gosh, yes. Those finds are absolute treasures. I think we'll have proof to extend."

"All right, I'll discuss it with your husband."

She grinned. "He's great at running this operation, Mom."

I smiled back. "Somehow, I think I'll approve."

* * *

My first few days were always filled with office work. I spent hours reviewing artifacts and summarizing the key highlights in various reports. Gone for me were the days of actual excavating. I missed those days. To continue receiving funding, I had to make sure the finds were substantial and museum quality.

I received the call from Bette and was glad for the interruption. She was still interested in seeing the site. I didn't ask if Jaimie might visit too. I invited her to visit the site on Friday. If all went well, I thought I would extend the invitation to Jane's post-wedding party.

I settled into Jane's old place. It was small, but much more comfortable than a hotel. Steven had called several times; I continued to ignore his messages. Well, not exactly. But I planned my return calls when I knew he was most likely unavailable. Or maybe he was avoiding my calls too. I also had a call from Clarence Higgins. I took that one.

After I greeted him, he said, "Hello Miss Mel. I thought I would reach your voicemail. I apologize for disturbing you in Australia."

"No bother, Clarence. Is there something you need to discuss?"

"Miss Mel, I must head back to Detroit for a few days. I should be back by the time you return. I am anxious to proceed with our project. When can we meet again?'

"I return a week from now. How about next Friday? Will you be back by then? Say, a seven o'clock dinner?"

"That'll be fine. Perfect. I might have more information for you as well. I've had some developments at home which I think will help."

"I hope it's good news?" Not sure if that comment even made sense.

"I'm not sure about good news," he admitted, "but helpful nonetheless."

The phone wasn't the way I wanted to learn more, so I quelled my curiosity. "Well, I'll take that as good news. See you soon, and please call if you need me."

"I will, Miss Mel. Thank you."

I clicked off and sent a note to Beverly to add Clarence to my schedule. I was suddenly looking forward to my return to the States.

Chapter 6

 *Washington, DC, 1933*

Edward tried to avoid the two men with flashy badges. One grabbed him by the arm.

"May we ask you a few questions?" the taller man said.

Edward continued to ignore them.

"Where are my manners? Let me introduce ourselves. I'm Detective Mahoney and this is my partner Detective McCarthy. What is this place?"

"Right now it's under construction, but soon enough it'll be a restaurant."

"A restaurant you say? Anything you'd like to add to that?" McCarthy asked.

"Not really. A restaurant. You know, where people eat food. Not much more explainin' to do for a restaurant."

"Come on, Mister—"

"Edward."

Mahoney's eyes became slits. "Come on, Edward. Don't fuck with us. You know what we're gettin' at. We've had our eye on this joint and it ain't just no eating place. I understand your boss, Hirsh Rosenburg, is runnin' the joint."

"Let's just say we know he ain't known for opening up fancy restaurants," McCarthy pushed.

"Look, Detectives," Edward looked each man in the eye, "all I got to say is this is a eatin' place, plain as that. Are we done here, cause I have a lot to do."

"Edward, let me make this simple for you to understand." Mahoney paused for effect. "It better be a restaurant without booze or gambling. Like I said, we know Mr. Rosenburg ain't known as no food connoisseur." Mahoney laughed, almost proud he knew the word. "You're free to go. But let me leave you with this. You see any illegal activity startin' up, we'd like to know." He handed Edward a card. "My friend," he patted him on the back, "that call just might save your neck."

Edward had dealt with the Feds before. No sense in telling Hirsh. Feds poking around wouldn't make a bit of difference to Hirsh. He watched them walk away and headed the opposite direction, toward Spades.

Edward had been threatened twice this morning. Not a good start to the day. He knew threats were part of the job. But it was getting old, or he was getting old. In either case, he hoped to make enough money to get out of this line of work. Even if booze became legal, he knew that Hirsh would keep the back room for gambling. The Mayflower Club would be an illegal joint long after Edward planned to leave.

Although Edward made it a habit to look around before entering any building, he approached Spades with an especially wary eye. He wasn't sure when he became paranoid about his surroundings, just that the precaution was now a part of his routine. He stood on the corner and watched light traffic come and go. After a while he lit a cigarette and continued to watch the building, leaning against a parked car. Seeing no imminent risk, he leisurely finished his cigarette, flicked it into the street, and walked toward Spades.

At the front door, not sure what to do, he knocked. No one answered, and he didn't hear anyone on the other side. He put his ear to the door. Hearing nothing, he slowly turned the handle and opened it. Hesitating, he stepped into the massive empty building. He had no idea where to go. To his right, he saw a staircase. He began to head toward the stairs when, from out of nowhere, he heard, "Password."

He gave the password to seemingly no one. Not knowing what to do next, he waited and then finally heard, "Come up the stairs." He obeyed, and saw one door at the end of a long hall. Pensive, he walked down the hall and reached the door, feeling somehow grateful he was still alive. At his knock, a tiny window opened. Edward gave the window the same password and the door creaked open.

"Where's Sammy?" he asked with all the courage he could muster.

The man, without saying a word, led him to Sammy's office. Sammy stood as Edward entered the room.

"Hello Edward. Hirsh said he was sending you. You know you shouldn't be in this part of town?" More statement than question.

"I'm fine, suh." Edward took the list out of his pocket. "Mr. Rosenburg, he say he needs this in six weeks." He handed Sammy the list.

"Sit down. Please sit down," Sammy motioned to a chair.

Edward took a seat, and while Sammy skimmed the list, he looked around the room. The window guard stood by the door. He had a shoulder holster with a Colt 1908 that was surely loaded. There was a tommy gun propped up in the corner and a rack of shotguns mounted on the wall. Edward did not want to be around should all these weapons be necessary. Just the thought made him impatient for this meeting to end. He turned his attention to Sammy.

He watched Sammy make several notes. Sammy put his pen down and looked back up. "When did you say you need the goods? Six weeks?"

"Yes suh."

Sammy looked back down at the list. "You tell Hirsh I'll have the goods ready for him. And tell him, he don't need to worry about me or the stuff. If he needs anything else, you just let ol' Sammy know. You want a ride back?"

"No suh. I'll be okay. No trouble gettin' here." The thought of a gangster driving him anywhere was not pleasant.

Sammy simply nodded. "Okay then. Tell Hirsh, I need the full amount in cash when I deliver. I need a back entrance and will only deliver early in the morning. Say about three a.m. Make sure he's clear on that. I'll be in touch."

"Yes, suh."

Edward stood and was accompanied to the door by the window guard. Without a word, the guard turned three locks, looked out the tiny window, and then opened the door.

Edward quickly walked down the hall and then down the stairs. As he exited the building, he put his hands together as if saying a prayer, looked up to the sky, and hoped he would never be back.

As he started walking in the direction of the club, he could feel the summer's midday heat beating down on his neck. He took off his jacket, slung it over his arm, and turned his thoughts to the mirror. The big mirror. How was he going to solve this? He'd visited every furniture store, hardware store, and glass manufacturer within five miles of the club, and left each shop with sympathetic apologies and promises to contact him if anything came up. And to make matters worse, he still had no leads for an artist. He decided to take a short walk over to Burstrom's Lumber. Maybe they might know somebody that could help. A long shot, but he was running out of options.

He was just about to turn onto Jersey Street when he heard a car slowing behind him. He picked up his pace.

The convertible pulled up alongside him. "Where ya goin'?" one of the men shouted. Another man said, "This ain't your part of town. You lost?"

"Need a ride?" the third man called out.

Edward ignored the men and kept moving while he quickly but casually surveyed the area. Seeing no traffic or people, he knew this would be trouble. He continued to walk.

"Did you hear us, boy?" the first one asked.

With an unexpected swerve the car stopped in front of him, blocking his path. He watched as one of the men got out of the car.

"I asked you once. Where you think you're going?"

"I ain't looking for no trouble." Edward looked the man in the eye. "Just goin' back to work."

"Oh yeah? You got a job? And where's that?"

"I ain't gotta tell you shit," he said in a low voice. Anger made his tone indignant. "Now get outta my way."

"Don't talk to me like that, boy."

Edward remembered the gun in his coat pocket. Easier to reach if he'd left his coat on. Now he wasn't sure which pocket it was in.

"Well since you don't know nothin', maybe we oughta show you about—"

"Look here," Edward said, fighting the slight quiver in his voice, "I said I don't want no trouble."

One of the men reached in the back of the car and pulled out a baseball bat. The other man grabbed a crowbar. "Then you should'a been more respectful. But I think it's too late for that now. Don't you think, Henry?"

"Why, I surely do. Let's teach this boy a lesson 'bout bein' respectful."

The baseball bat hit Edward squarely in the back. He grabbed his back and fell to the ground. He dropped his coat and the revolver slid out of his pocket and out of reach. He attempted to stagger back up and just as one of the men went for his revolver, Edward heard a click.

"My friend here don't want you boys botherin' him, do you Edward?" Hirsh had his .38 Special targeted at one man's head.

"They ain't botherin' me, boss. Just a bunch of no-accounts."

"Is that true? You're not botherin' my friend here?'

"No sir. We was just having a friendly conversation, weren't we, uh, Edward."

Edward made it to his feet and snatched the gun off the ground. "They ain't worth it, boss."

Hirsh pointed his gun at the man with the baseball bat. "Get your fat asses back in the car. I see any of you peckerheads again, I promise I'll blow your fuckin' brains out."

"Whoa. Take it easy old man." One of the men said this with his hands symbolically in the air. "We weren't hurtin' nobody. At least not yet." All three men looked in Edward's direction. "What you protectin' a negro for anyway? Not a good idea 'round here."

With Hirsh's gun still pointed at them, one man opened the car door, and the three men climbed back in.

Edward watched them get back in the car. As they drove off laughing, he said, "I could'a handled them, boss."

"Not from where I was lookin'."

"I could'a handled it boss. They weren't nothin'."

"Look Edward. I got to thinkin' you were runnin' late. Let's just say I came at an opportune time. You hurt?" He touched Edward's back and Edward couldn't stop the wince.

"I'll be okay, boss."

"I need you to stay outta trouble. The club don't need no distractions right now."

"I know, boss. I know," Edward said quietly.

"Get back to the club and keep an eye on things. I don't trust none of them when I'm away. They probably ain't doin' shit."

"Yes, boss. I'll keep an eye out."

"Everything go okay at Spades?"

"I asked for six weeks and Sammy said he could deliver. Money upfront, early morning drop."

"Good. Good work. You sure you're okay?"

"They didn't get me that bad," Edward lied. "I won't let that happen again. I'll keep a better look out."

"See that it doesn't."

"Yes boss."

Hirsh watched Edward walk away with a slight limp. Once Edward was out of view, he turned around and headed to the liquor distributor.

While he walked, Hirsh thought. Maybe he should've left Edward behind after the last joint was raided. Edward had always been a liability, but never to this extent. There was a trust factor between them. Hirsh couldn't deny that. But now he was seeing the burden a little clearer. He would continue to keep an eye out for him, but not at the expense of the club.

Decision made, he turned his thoughts to the problem at hand, his meeting with Pete LeBeck. Serving low-quality booze was unthinkable. Which meant paying premium prices. Added to that, payoffs and bribes had never been higher. He had to pay off the distributor, and the distributor paid the mob. The higher up the chain, the costlier the bribe. Liquor distributors never showed loyalty to customers, either. No need to. Especially LeBeck, who provided top-shelf-quality liquor. Bribing LeBeck wasn't necessarily the problem. Inventory was. Maybe LeBeck would have better news about that today.

* * *

LeBeck's wasn't easy to find. Hirsh pulled out a piece of paper with the address and peered at it. Not being familiar with where he was, he assumed he was at least close. Liquor distributors were usually tucked away in a shady, seedy part of town … for a reason … but after several wrong turns, Hirsh was becoming agitated. At last he found the street, and walked down to a dilapidated old building resembling a barn. There was no number on the building, but the markers Pete LeBeck provided him matched where he was standing. He looked to his left and right, to make sure he wasn't followed, and then knocked on an old splintered brown door.

"Password," Hirsh heard through the door.

"Rainy days," Hirsh replied.

The door opened. Two goons, both with guns, big guns, greeted him.

Somewhat unsettled, yet staying confident, Hirsh asked, "Where's Pete?"

One of the men stayed at the door and Hirsh followed the second to LeBeck's office.

"So when ya opening?" LeBeck asked.

"When can you supply the quantities we discussed, Pete?" Hirsh countered.

"Well it's like this. Chicago and New York are takin' everything. I'm tryin' to get my share, but DC, ain't the big market like them."

"Look, Pete. I'd tell you I can take my business elsewhere, but we both know, that ain't happenin'. My options are limited." No sense in pretending the supply was better elsewhere. It wasn't. "I open in less than eight weeks. Opening the restaurant sooner, but need the liquor in seven."

"What's it worth to ya?" LeBeck asked.

"I'm already paying five percent above what you asked."

"Pay me eight, I'll see what I can do."

"Jesus H. Christ, Pete, you said five!"

"Don't fuck with me, Hirsh. You'll be swimmin' in dough. You know it. The DC, cops are lazy. Those dickheads in Washington don't know their arse from a hole in the ground. The mayor's an Irish prick, and every cathouse in town stays in business because no one's looking. What they got is gobs of dough. Whores and dough. Eight percent, and I'll have what you need in seven weeks."

Hirsh looked down. He had no choice. But he continued to sit there, staring at the floor without speaking.

Irritated, LeBeck said, "What'll it be? I'm busy."

"Alright, alright. Seven weeks, Pete. Have it ready. We got a deal. Eight percent. That's it."

"Give me a list and I'll have it delivered."

Hirsh pulled a list from his shirt pocket. "I only need the good stuff. None of the bathtub gin shit." Hirsh was determined to exert *some* confidence in this meeting. "Don't fuck with me on this, Pete. Clientele's too important."

LeBeck looked at the list and then back up at Hirsh. "Don't lecture me. I'll have what you need." And with that, the meeting was over. LeBeck nodded to the guard with the gun and Hirsh was escorted to the door.

As Hirsh left LeBeck's, he thought long and hard about increasing his prices. The nation was still reeling from the Depression, but DC, wasn't as affected as the rest of the country. LeBeck was right about the politicians. They'd be at his club, boozing and gambling. No need to worry, he decided. Jack up the prices. It wouldn't stop anyone from coming to the Mayflower Club.

Hirsh turned the corner onto Connecticut Avenue. Out of the corner of his eye, he saw two men staring at the club. It wasn't long before they began to look his way. Feds already casing the joint, he decided. He looked right at them, smiled, tipped his hat, and opened the door to the club.

George was standing near the entrance and spotted him. "Millie's here."

He completely forgot he was meeting his wife for a late lunch. He walked around the corner and saw her standing by the stairs.

"Don't tell me you forgot again?" she whined, hands on her hips.

"Millie, of course not. I cut my meetin' short just to be with you," he lied.

Hirsh had been married to Millie for a few years now. She'd been one of the showgirls at his last club. Light on brains, but strong on looks. Six feet tall with legs that never stopped. Blond curly hair that stopped right at the top of her large breasts. Millie appreciated the money he provided and showed her loyalty with frequent, kinky sex. Unlike other women who flaunted themselves in front of Hirsh, Millie was worth keeping happy. At least for now.

"Oh darlin', I know you're busy, what with all the work goin' on here." Millie emphasized her words by blindly looking around the club as she spoke.

He walked over to her, grabbed her by the waist, and kissed her on the cheek. "Millie, my love, this is all for you," he whispered in her ear, "give me a minute and we'll head out."

He glanced around until he found Edward and pulled him aside. "I think I saw a couple gumshoes near the entrance. You see them before?"

"No boss, can't say's I have," Edward lied. Too late to tell him now.

"Watch the place."

"Yes, boss."

Hirsh took Millie's hand and headed for the front entrance. Let the Feds take a look around he thought. He wasn't worried.

* * *

Edward was about to head upstairs when he heard the phone ring. The club was in such disarray he forgot where the phone was, but finally found it under several sheets of construction paper.

"Mayflower Club."

"Ah, hello. Is Edward there?" A timid voice on the other end.

"Speakin'," Edward said, pain making his reply gruff.

"Hi. My name is Billy. Billy Wade. I understand from a friend of mine that you're looking for an artist to sketch on a mirror? A rather large mirror?"

"Yeah."

"Well, I might be able to help. I'm a sketch artist lookin' for work. I can provide references, and I'll work for a reasonable rate."

"We'll decide what's reasonable."

"Fair enough, for now anyway. Can I come by and see this mirror?"

"Here's the thing. It's not here yet. Do this. I need a sketch—on a large piece of paper—of a girl lookin' sexy. Big smile. And I need the name of the club, 'The Mayflower Club,' sketched on it too. Bring it by tomorrow. We'll look at your work."

"Are you going to pay me for the sketch?"

"No, we ain't. You guys are a dime a dozen. If we like your work, you're hired. It's up to you."

"Hmm. Let me think about it. If I agree, I'll be by tomorrow with a sketch. What time should I come by? If I do at all."

"Be here at noon. The boss will want to see the sketch. Ask for Edward."

"Okay, noon. If I come at all."

He needed this guy. Maybe he shouldn't have been so rough. This day wasn't getting any better.

Chapter 7

 Los Angeles, 2015

As I made my way to the airport, I found myself surprised at all I accomplished on this trip. I was able to extend the contract at Devil's Lair for two more years. On the strength of that deal, I hired another archeologist and best yet, closed a new contract in Sydney. Small, but it would help. My accountant had reminded me that my bank account was still on shaky ground. I hated reality checks but decided after our discussion to expand my company in other directions. On the flip side, my own daughter hadn't seen the need to include me in her wedding plans. Although the party was a big success, I spent most evenings working, and I never saw Jaimie again. Okay, the Jaimie part was the most depressing. To top that off, when I arrived back in LA, I'd have to dump Steven.

My semi good mood turned sour. I began to question the Steven decision. He seemed to care about me and was certainly a charmer. Was he all that bad? And I didn't have proof he was cheating, just a good hunch. We'd only been dating for a few years. Maybe my expectations were too high.

What was wrong with me? I wasn't thinking clearly about Steven. Maybe if we took a vacation. Maybe ... I saw my phone light up.

"G'day Melinda, it's Jaimie. I understand from my sister that you're leaving today," he said sounding disappointed, or was it my imagination?

I could barely put a coherent sentence together.

"Hi Jaimie," I stammered. "Why yes I, I'm on the way to the airport now." Why did this guy make me lose my ability to speak?

"It wasn't my intention to miss seeing you again. The contract with Warner Brothers may be saved after all, and it took too much time to negotiate. I was hoping the three of us could get together for dinner before you left."

"I, ah, well, certainly understand. Such a big contract and all." I had nothing else.

"As it turns out, I'm coming to Los Angeles on Friday. I'd like to hear more about what you do. Running an archeology company sounds intriguing. Would it be possible that you and I could meet for dinner Saturday evening?"

"Why, um, yes. That would be just fine."

"Aces! I'll call you when I arrive. And Melinda ... I look forward to seeing you."

"Wonderful. See you Saturday," I managed. "And good luck with the negotiations."

Just the way he'd said my name—Mel-*lin*-da—made me want to give up my nickname for good. If my heart were beating any faster, it would explode. At my age, to be so incoherent, witless ... I'd be having one stiff cocktail before that dinner.

After I hung up the phone, my mind drifted back to Steven. Dumping him suddenly became much more attractive. Why was I reconsidering in the first place? I forgot!

My flight back to Los Angeles was an overnight flight. I'd never been able to sleep well on planes. My overhead light was the only one on. Between Jaimie and Clarence Higgins, two such disparate subjects, my mind was too wired to think clearly about either. I tried reading but couldn't concentrate. Working was out of the question. I glanced at the same magazine several times with no comprehension of what I was leafing through and watched a forgettable movie or two. Before I knew it, we were landing.

As I opened the door to my apartment, I was greeted by Allen, who had Poodles on a leash.

"Hello Ms. Danbury. Welcome back. Abby said you'd be back today. Let me get your bags. By the way, there's a guy waiting for you in the kitchen."

Shaking my head, I wheeled in my rolling suitcase and let my carry-on plop to the floor. I gave Poodles a pat on the head and looked back up at Allen. "Would his name be Steven?"

"I think so. Abby and I were just heading out to walk the dog."

"Mom! You're back," Abby said in genuine excitement.

As I hugged her, I saw Steven coming through the kitchen's french doors.

Abby looked in Steven's direction. Then looked at me. "Allen and I were just heading out. We'll catch up later. Bye, Steven."

"Bye guys," Steven responded.

As Abby and Allen passed by me out the door, Steven walked toward me and gave me a gentle hug. "Hi, honey. You must be exhausted. I just stopped by to make you a vodka martini and I brought dinner from Roscoe's."

Roscoe's. Our favorite Italian restaurant. Was his kindness out of love or guilt? I chose guilt.

"Let's sit down," I said. We headed for the living room, and before I lost my nerve, I started the heart-breaking as soon as we settled onto the sofa, martinis in hand.

"Steven, please don't think what I'm about to say in any way relates to my exhaustion from a sixteen-hour flight." I took a gulp of the martini. "I'm not gonna drag this out either. We both know this relationship has been hit-and-miss for a while now.

"Steven, honestly, I don't have the time to keep our relationship afloat. Or—" a sigh that wasn't all that dramatic— "or the desire. I should, I know. But I simply don't care to. Before we put more time and effort into this, I needed to tell you that." I waited, mulling over my only regret, which was what a truly fine martini Steven could make.

Since no reply was forthcoming and the only response a blank stare, I continued. "Don't hate me for this. Or maybe hating is good. I don't know. But it's been on my mind for months, and I can't function or continue my life happily with you in it." That last part sounded a little harsh, but the words were out there.

Steven stared at the floor for maybe half a minute, looked back up at me, and finally put a sentence together. "Look, I'm not shocked with this, but I always felt we could, I don't know, make it work. We make such a great couple. I thought we enjoyed each other's company. I was happy with that."

Now I was more convinced that this was the best decision. Even his argument for staying together was mind-numbing. And then he added, "But before either of us becomes too miserable and we begin to see other people, I'd like to think that time away might spark something. Some sort of reason on both our parts."

Technically, I wasn't seeing anyone else. I still believed Steven had a little something on the side. I held to that thought as surely as I held my ground.

"I understand what you're saying," I said. Even though I didn't. "I can't think this might work itself out. It's like a vase that shatters into hundreds of pieces. Not only is gluing it back together a lot of work, but it also won't look the same. I'm not up for the work. I know this sounds shallow and maybe even lazy, but please believe me, I've put a lot of thought into this."

He gave a weak smile. "That's one of your problems, hon. You put a lot of thought into everything. It's also why I care about you. If you're expecting me to yell and scream and beg, you know that's not me."

I did know this and realized the lack of emotion was part of the problem. But no sense in addressing that now. "I know that's not your way, Steven. And I respect that."

He leaned back against the sofa cushion, one knee clasped between his hands. "Okay. Look. I'm not going to sit by my phone and wait for your call. And I know that being friends is cliché, and might not happen, but as time passes and you want a night out, call. I'm not saying I'll answer," he paused, maybe hoping I'd interject hope, "but I won't cuss you out, either."

"We're not sixteen, Steven. This is painful for us both. Please don't think I'll call. But I do appreciate the offer."

I was too jetlagged and sleep-deprived to keep this sad event continuing. I stood. "Let me walk you out."

Walking to the door, Steven took my hand. I didn't resist. We stopped in front of the door, where he looked at me and gallantly kissed my hand. He then kissed me on the cheek and with one last, long glance into each other's eyes, he turned the knob, opened the door, and walked out.

With the lights on, Roscoe's Italian waiting for me in the kitchen, and suitcases by the door, I went to my bedroom and with tears streaming down my cheeks, collapsed on the bed.

* * *

I awoke to a knock on the bedroom door. Sunlight streaming in from the window. Disoriented, I saw Abby walk into the room.

"You've been asleep for almost ten hours, Mom. Just making sure you're not dead."

I bit off my laughter when I saw a genuine concerned look on her face.

Seeing that I was still alive, she turned back into the daughter I knew so well. "Allen and I ate the Italian food. Hope you weren't planning on having any today. He tried to hold me back, but it was pointless." Trying to redeem herself, she followed with, "Make you some breakfast before I go to class?"

"Thank you, no," I mumbled.

"How'd it go with Steven?"

I shook my head to clear it. "I, we broke up. Not easy, but it's done." I felt a sudden surge of regret and melancholy. Where'd that come from?

As if Abby picked up on this she said, "Mom he's a great guy, I'm not gonna lie. But you're a great person too. There doesn't have to be a reason to be miserable in a relationship. Sometimes you just are."

"Reasons seem to make it easier, but I appreciate the thought. Anyway, thanks for getting me going."

"How was your trip? Shocked about Jane getting married? She's not pregnant, is she?"

"Trip was good. Shocked about the wedding, and as far as I know she is not pregnant. Happy too. I could tell she felt bad about not including us in the plans. But we had a nice party, and I do like William. This puts pressure on you though. I'd like a big wedding from one of my girls."

"Funny. Very funny. No comment or commitment from me," Abby said as she left the bedroom.

I slowly processed the day ahead of me. Work from home, definitely. My brain was too tired to accomplish anything significant, and I could rifle through paperwork at home. I remembered again that Steven and I were through. Sad, but a relief as well. I dragged myself out of bed, threw on my bathrobe and moseyed to the kitchen to make coffee. As I entered the kitchen, I noticed that the kids tidied up after themselves. Must've been Allen's doing.

My phone rang. Thinking it was Steven, surprised to be disappointed that it wasn't. Give it time, Mel, I told myself.

"Miss Mel, it's Clarence Higgins. I'll be back from Detroit day after tomorrow," he stated without pleasantries. "Are we still scheduled to meet on Friday?"

"Hello Clarence, I'll check," I tried to slow him down. "How is seven at Roscoe's?" The only restaurant I could think of and regretted as soon as I said it. "Not far from the office, it's just—"

"I will find it. See you then. Thank you and sorry for the rush."

I wasn't sure what to make of his rush, but the meeting gave me something to look forward to. More a diversion. What could Clarence be so worked up about?

Chapter 8

Washington, DC, 1933

A young man wearing a Yankees baseball cap, dungarees and a clean, pressed white shirt stood outside the Mayflower Club, clutching a drawing he hoped would change his life. He'd stayed up all night working on the drawing and now, seeing the club, his confidence grew.

As he opened the door, Billy was overwhelmed by the sheer size of the restaurant. The ceiling was at least thirty-feet-high. He turned the corner and noticed a grand staircase on the right that led to a second-floor balcony. New wood flooring was being installed, and massive booths were under construction on the right side, behind the staircase. On the left he noticed what looked like a bar being built, and behind it was a wall that his artist's eye judged to at least twenty feet high. *That must be where the mirror will be placed.*

"Can I help ya?" Edward asked.

"My name is Billy Wade." He saw no instant recognition. "The artist that called about the mirror?"

"Oh yeah, yeah," Edward said. "Let me get Mr. Rosenburg."

Edward walked up the stairs and knocked on Hirsh's office door.

"The guy with the mirror drawin' is here."

"He any good?" Hirsh snapped.

"Don't know. Haven't looked at what he brought."

"Be right down."

"Yes boss."

As Edward walked down the stairs, he noticed Billy looking at the wall where the mirror would go. Billy's hands were raised up and formed an open square, through which he seemed to be peering.

Billy noticed Edward's curiosity and grinned. "Just checking the drawing to the size of the wall."

Edward had no idea what that meant. He just hoped the drawing was good. Could be one less detail for him to worry over.

Hirsh made his way down the stairs. Edward pointed out Billy and Hirsh walked toward him.

"Young man, I understand you have a drawing you'd like me to look at?" Hirsh said with unusual kindness in his voice.

"Yes sir. If I could just use one of your tables to show you the drawing."

Hirsh directed him to one of the tables under construction, picked up an abandoned rag and cleared away the dust, and Billy slowly unveiled the drawing. The words

"The Mayflower Club" were at the top of the drawing in a perfectly drawn slanted-letter design. Below the words was the most beautiful woman Hirsh had ever seen. She was sitting in a martini glass with a cup in one hand and, in a somewhat suggestive manner, holding a stirring stick. Short, curly hair, blouse unbuttoned so you could just begin to see her ample cleavage, a short playful skirt, and a seductive, sexy smile.

Billy saw the delight on Hirsh's face. He'd seen that look before. Billy knew he was talented, but the Depression had him sleeping on the streets. The feeling washed over him that it was all about to change.

Hirsh studied the drawing for a few minutes, and in a flash, his approval disappeared, replaced by the Hirsh everyone else saw every day.

"Now son, this is a good renderin' of what I'm looking for. Let's just say I may even like what I see. It's not perfect, but I might be able to work with it." Hirsh spoke while scratching his chin. "What would it cost to etch somethin' like this on a mirror? There's lots'a detail here."

Billy realized what was going on. Hirsh wanted the drawing, but he wanted to pay bottom dollar. This was a nice club. Nicest he'd ever stepped foot in. The exposure alone could warrant some negotiating. Billy needed the work. He wanted to nail this down now.

"If I cut back on the detail, it won't look near as good." He stopped for a minute, looked at the drawing and then back at Hirsh. "Tell you what I'll do." From his portfolio, he withdrew a scrap of paper and wrote down a price, then showed it to Hirsh.

"Son, I can't pay that. You're out of your mind if you think I'd pay that much money!"

The number was high, but that was part of the plan. "Tell you what I'll do," Billy said. "If you let me work here, part time, and mention my name to anyone interested in the mirror, I'll charge you half."

Hirsh thought for a moment. "I see what you're doing here …" He pointed to the front door for effect. "I should tell ya to walk out those doors. I'm not stupid." As if expecting a denial, Hirsh said no more.

A long minute passed. Billy stayed quiet, the confident silence borne of knowing that the man *wanted* this drawing.

Hirsh broke first. "Tell you what I'll do. I don't know 'bout your ability to work in a club, but I'll give you thirty days to prove you can help around here. When the mirror gets here," he looked at Edward with slight frustration, "you'll need to start on that."

Billy smiled. "It's risky on my part, but I think we can make the arrangement work."

"We have a deal." Hirsh shook his hand. He glared at Edward. "It's up to you to find the mirror—"

"I think I can help with that too," Billy interjected. "One of the art suppliers I deal with might just have a solution."

Edward knew nothing about art. Hopefully, Billy could solve his problem. This damn mirror hunting had kept him awake at night.

Edward looked at Billy. "Can we go look now? I need to get this done. Boss here is itchin' for this mirror. Can't say why it's so important."

Billy shrugged. "Let's take a walk. It's not far."

Edward swiveled his head toward Hirsh. "Be back in a few minutes, boss."

"Take longer if it means getting this done," Hirsh said as Billy and Edward headed toward the door.

* * *

Hirsh walked to the back of the restaurant. It had been four weeks since construction started, and progress was slow. And the setbacks galled him every time he thought about them. A set of pipes broke and leaked water from the second floor to the first floor, damaging a large portion of the newly installed oak floor beyond repair. The bar chairs had to be sent back, and two of his best construction workers were arrested for robbing a grocery store. The phone rang.

"Mayflower Club," George said. A few seconds rolled by. "Just a minute, I'll get him for ya. Hirsh, it's for you," he bellowed, holding the receiver in the air.

Hirsh walked to the bar and yanked the receiver out of George's hand, making a mental note to teach George how to properly answer a phone. "Yes, can I help ya?"

"Mr. Rosenburg, my name is Mrs. Irene Butler. Good day to you."

"Good day, ma'am," Hirsh said, impatiently tapping his fingers on the bar.

"I was curious when the club might be opening?"

"We don't have an exact date yet, ma'am. Maybe a few more weeks. But if you call back—"

"Let me tell you the reason for my call," she cut Hirsh off. "I have an interested party that might want to visit."

"Well that's just fine," Hirsh started again. "As I said—"

"Let's just say this interested party might want to bring a few guests, mainly to have dinner."

Mainly to have dinner. Hirsh had heard that phrase before. And usually from high-placed individuals.

Hirsh made his tone more polite. "If I may have your telephone number, I'd be happy to call you when we're close to opening."

"No. That's fine. I'll call back. In a few weeks you say?"

"Yes, ma'am. Maybe three."

"I hope it's not much later," she stated and hung up the phone.

Hirsh blankly stared at the receiver, more eager than ever to open the Mayflower Club. Already the word was getting around, and already, there were high-class paying guests interested. Just like he'd hoped.

Chapter 9

 *Los Angeles, 2015*

I arrived at Roscoe's early. "On time" is late for me. I didn't see Clarence Higgins at the entrance. I did see Tony, the owner of Roscoe's, and mentioned I was waiting for a client. I asked for a booth and as I walked to the table, I felt a tap on my shoulder followed by "Mel."

I turned around to see Steven and a young girl. Maybe a young woman, but either way, the emphasis was on *young*.

"Hello Steven." I shook his hand while looking at the girl next to him. She was obviously from wealth. The tight-fitting white Chanel dress along with red Jimmy Choo shoes and bag to match seemed like overkill for Roscoe's, but who was I to judge? I looked back at Steven as he began to speak.

"Mel, this is Justine." His eyes held mine as he put his arm around her. I should've known better than to come to Roscoe's.

"Hello, ma'am," Justine said as she shook my hand.

I gave her that one. "Justine, you look to be about my daughter's age. Do you go to college around here?" Not original, but I didn't care.

Steven gave a sarcastic look, but Justine carried on with no sign of indignation. "As a matter of fact I do. I'm working on my master's degree in economics. I feel fortunate to have landed a fellowship at UCLA." Steven proudly smirked. I'd give her that one too.

"Well I hope that Steven is a good mentor for you," I said. Not a great comeback. And I seemed to be on shaky ground here. Best to wrap this up before I made more of a fool of myself. "I'm meeting a client and must get to my table." I waved a symbolic goodbye.

I did break up with the guy, but it didn't mean I had a heart of stone. Still somewhat reeling from that unfortunate exchange, I noticed Clarence heading my way. Since we last met, he'd obviously acclimated to the Southern California weather—and its style. Tonight he wore a crisply tailored over-the-waist shirt, in white with a tiny gold print, over pressed casual slacks. No derby to cover his tightly curled, graying hair, and he'd swapped the overcoat for a light, loose sports jacket. His ever-present cane was the only jarring note. He greeted me with a firm handshake.

"I hope that your trip to Australia was successful, Miss Mel?" More a statement than a question.

"What ... oh ... yes, Clarence, it was."

We walked to our table and Giovanni, my favorite waiter, asked what we'd like to drink. I ordered a dry martini. I thought about a double, but this was a working dinner. Clarence ordered tea and as soon as Giovanni left, he proceeded to tell his long-awaited story.

"Thank you, Miss Mel, for meeting with me. I do apologize for my rushed manner on the phone the other day. I had a bit of bad news from home, which may pertain to this meeting, but I'll save for later. Now ... let me start from the beginning. There are some gaps in the story, but I will do my best. How familiar are you with Prohibition?"

"Prohibition? Same as the next person, I guess. The 18th Amendment, was it? Might not have the number right, but it prohibited drinking in the twenties and early thirties. I think. Am I good so far?"

"That is a good start. I didn't even know that much until I got involved in all this. The 18th Amendment prohibited the manufacture and sale of alcohol, with a few exceptions, but the Volstead Act enforced the amendment. In other words, if you were caught drinking, you were in violation of the Volstead Act. And if you were caught making liquor, you were in violation of the 18th Amendment."

"I see." I gave him an apologetic smile. "I guess my history knowledge is somewhat ... deficient."

"You know more than most. Half the people in this restaurant couldn't tell you which amendment Prohibition falls under. I only share this with you because it's one of the reasons why I'm here."

Giovanni brought our drinks and asked if we'd like to order. We did, and with that out of the way, Clarence continued.

"I have an uncle who died in 1972. He lived in Detroit, and after his death and until fairly recently, we rented the house he'd lived in to numerous tenants. When I became older, I was the one who oversaw the property, met with the tenants, and managed the house. The family trusted me, but" he chuckled, "it wasn't a role I was very good at. Unfortunately, there was no one else willin' to take it on, so the responsibility fell on me.

"The last tenant moved out recently, and I don't want to keep renting it. I decided to put the house up for sale. I'd like to retire, you see, and my share from selling would help me with that. The house needs a lot of work, though. Some of the flooring needed to be replaced, along with bathroom remodeling, and roof repair. I had quite a list. One of the companies that came to give me an estimate seemed to spend a lot of time on the third floor. I thought I recognized him as one of the tenants, but there were so many, I wasn't sure. I decided to check on him and went upstairs. I got there in time to see the fellow taking something out of the floor. And thought I saw him put something in his pocket but couldn't be sure.

"I asked him what he was doing. At that point he had to show me the loose board. There was some scattered paper underneath and a long, thin, tin box. I didn't know what it was, but acted like I did, and explained that it was nothing but family pictures."

"Did he believe you?" I asked.

"I'm not sure. I know I should've asked him if he took anything, but it all happened so fast. I told him I was late for an appointment, that he'd have to come back and finish later. I never called him back—and he never contacted me about finishing the quote."

"What was in the box?"

"That's why I wanted to meet with you. I got in there after he left. Inside the box is a lot of paperwork. It all seems disjointed to me, but it mentions a club, actually a restaurant, in Washington, DC, called 'The Mayflower Club.' Apparently, the Mayflower Club was a speakeasy in the 1930s that offered illegal liquor and gambling. Anyway, what little I could find out, the Mayflower Club isn't there anymore, but the building is. It's a restaurant called now. I've been several times, mostly to look around and see what kind of place it is. There's a lot more history about the building, but that's for a later conversation."

I listened, but my focus was on something much smaller than a building. "Anything else in the box?"

"Sorry, I'm getting to that. Like I said, some of it didn't make sense to me, but the paperwork kinda suggests something is hidden in the club: the building, I'm guessing. It doesn't say where. It's like my uncle was in the middle of trying to figure it out too when he passed."

"Does it say what it is? What's hidden there, I mean."

Clarence nodded. "A box with money. A lot of money."

I grabbed up my martini and leaned back in the chair. "How do you know that?"

While I sipped, Clarence gave his answer in the rushed speech I was beginning to realize was how he always spoke when excited. "I don't know for sure about why I think there's money in the box, but when I was ten or eleven, my uncle would tell stories about a club he worked at. And he always claimed he was rich. And that the money was stashed somewhere. We all thought he was senile and paid him no attention. He was always going to find it, or was just about to go and retrieve it, but he died without ever doing anything like that. He'd mentioned the Mayflower Club, but we never looked it up. Like I said, we thought he was just an old man makin' stuff up. He said he and another guy named Hirsh Rosenburg ran the club. Black folk in the thirties didn't run anything, especially a fancy club. We all forgot about it, and of course back then people didn't keep records like they do nowadays … none of us thought it was worth the trouble to check on what he said."

Our food arrived, and in the thrall of heaping plates of pasta and sauce that made Roscoe's the hottest Italian food place in town, it was several minutes before we picked up the conversation. I drained my martini glass and held it up. Giovanni responded to the call, and while he did, I leaned back and regarded Clarence's light-pecan eyes studying my paler ones, and the fact that his plate was mostly untouched and his beverage choice had remained iced tea. "So … you said you and your relatives decided it wasn't worth investigating your uncle's story. By contacting me, I take it to mean that you changed your mind?"

Though tired, his smile made his face brighten, and in that moment, he looked younger.

"I searched the internet as best I could," he said, "and sure enough, it says my uncle Edward was involved in that club. Just not sure how."

"And how can I help you exactly?"

"I'm asking you to come with me to Detroit and take a look at the box."

"If that's what you wanted from me, why not bring the box with you?"

The lightness left his face. "I could've brought it, but I was afraid to travel with it. I feel like someone's after me. Maybe that guy who came to bid and never showed up again. My other families never mentioned it again, but me, I can't quit wonderin'. What if I never get a chance to find out if what my uncle said was true?

"And it ain't only the box. I need your help with the internet. I mean, with the research. I'll pay for your time and expenses, and a percent of what we find. If there is anything to find. I can't guarantee any money or anything valuable will be found, but if you could at least go with me to Detroit, you can decide if you want to spend more time on this."

I thought while Clarence continued.

"I'd also like you to meet Dorothy, that's Hirsh Rosenburg's granddaughter."

I stopped thinking and paid heed to every word. Clarence noticed.

"When I found the name on the internet, I remembered hearing it before, from my uncle. Uncle Edward was convinced Dorothy knew where the money was hidden. She lives in an old folks' home now. Dorothy's mama and daddy, George, and Cecelia, came from Detroit, you see. And that's where Hirsh and my uncle met." Clarence paused for a moment as if looking for the right words.

He continued. "Dorothy eventually wound up back in Detroit. I hired a private investigator and he found her in the old folks' home. I've been to visit her. She won't talk. Which makes me believe there's something to what my uncle said."

I tried to take it all in. "Clarence … if you have other family, what are they say—"

His vigorous shake of his head stopped me. "What if Uncle Edward was just talking, what if there's nothing to anything he said? I don't trust the rest of the family until I know what I have. I could use your help, Miss Mel."

Steven walked past our table. He nodded in my direction and I did my best to ignore him.

I took another gulp of the martini. This was certainly different from my usual work. *But it's related, isn't it? Finding old stuff, old secrets?* Or maybe I just needed intrigue at this point in my life. Or maybe it was because I liked Clarence and liked to help people I liked. I decided to at least check out Detroit.

"Clarence, I'll tell you what I can do. This may be a wild goose chase, but I'm intrigued. My calendar is … somewhat open next week. I can meet you in Detroit on Monday, and then we can take it from there." The martini glass was nearly empty, but I didn't signal Giovanni this time, just placed it on the table between us, and leaned forward. "But before I say yes, is there anything else I need to know? Anything you might have … forgotten to share with me?"

"There is one last thing I haven't told you," he said. "That dead man I told you about the first time we met?"

I searched my memory, found that one, and nodded.

"Best knowledge I have, he worked at the old Mayflower Club. I believe there's something buried with him."

Interesting. But while I'd dug up plenty of bodies, I had a feeling digging up one that recent was going to be a problem. "Buried with him? Why do you say that? Isn't it illegal to dig up a dead guy?"

For the first time, his eyes shifted away.

"Miss Mel, I want to answer your question. I do. I'd feel terrible if I didn't tell you something you need to know now. But there's still much I don't know. I could spend the next two weeks right here, talkin', and I still might miss something you're askin' for. But I'll try. First we have to find out where he's buried. One of the pieces of paper in the box had a map. To a gravesite. But I know the area …" With a sigh, he returned his gaze to mine. "Main thing is, Uncle Edward believed that Dorothy knows where the money is. And somehow, it's related to where this guy is buried. Can we wait for me to say more when we're in Detroit? Maybe once we're there, I can sort out what you need to know a little better."

His words sounded right, but didn't feel right. "Why can't you tell me everything before—"

He held up a silencing hand. "Something else you oughta know now. And it'll explain the reason I sound like I'm in a hurry. My daughter's been staying at Uncle Edward's house, to keep an eye out until I can sell it. While you were gone, she phoned to tell me that a man's been coming around the house, acting like he's thinking about buying it, but not really. I asked her to describe him, and he might be the guy that was looking at the floors that day. I don't know what to make of it. But I don't believe in coincidences, Miss Mel. I've had a hard life and learned that there's no such thing. I'm heading back to Detroit tomorrow. If I see that guy I'm calling the police. But I really need you there on Monday."

I reached for the martini glass and held it up. "While I can't tell you exactly what to do, you have hired me. And yes, I'll work on this case. First opinion: I'd hold off on the police. Next: Let's say your suspicions are accurate. Where is the tin box?"

"In my bank," Clarence said as Giovanni returned.

"Okay. Good. As far as we know, he can't get any more important details or items from your house. So let him snoop around. Especially after you get back to Detroit. And especially once I make it there. Maybe we can find out what he knows. If he knows anything, which I doubt. If he does, and we can confirm a threat, then it might be time to involve the police."

"Okay Miss Mel. I'll take your advice," he grinned, "now that you're working for me."

I grinned right back. "Good."

We discussed a few more details while I finished the martini, exchanged departing pleasantries, and as I watched Clarence leave, I sincerely had no idea how I might be able to help, just that I wanted to. It was the weekend, and I could have flown to Detroit with him, but doing so meant I'd have to cancel my date with Jaimie. No sense in canceling a date.

After our meeting, I drove home, and, once in my office, started up my computer. I decided to do a little detective work. Clarence Higgins checked out okay, at least no arrest records or warrants. I typed in "The Mayflower Club" next, and a few articles popped up. Most mentioned that it was a speakeasy or "gin joint" as they were often called in the 1930s. Looked like this particular gin joint was popular with the locals, including politicians. Somewhat interesting, but not much help in the articles. After a few minutes I determined that I'd be putting in some library time. Looking at microfiche wasn't my idea of amusement, but I needed copies of the *Washington Times* and *Washington Post* from the thirties. There was also an African-American newspaper called the *Afro-American* that might yield some information. I looked up the address of the main Washington, DC, library and felt like I was formulating some sort of plan.

I closed the computer and found myself becoming anxious about my date with Jaimie. As I turned off the lights, I noticed my phone glowing. I'd forgotten to turn the ringer back on after the meeting.

"Hi Mel, it's Jaimie," I heard a commotion in the background. "I'll have to cancel our plans for tomorrow. My dad had a heart attack and I'm on my way back to Australia."

"Oh no, I'm so sorry. I … is there anything I can do for you?" I muttered, expecting a "no thank you."

"As a matter of fact there is. I would be ever so grateful if you could help me with a few things in my apartment. I'm terribly sorry to ask, but to catch this flight I had to leave without stopping by the place. There's a document that needs to be delivered to Warner Brothers Monday morning. It's in my office, plainly marked. I promise you can't miss it. My assistant is on vacation and I can't reach anyone else. The front desk can give you a key to the place and I'll send you the contact info for Warner Brothers. Is this too much to ask? I know we hardly know each other, but as a fellow business owner …"

"It's not too much to ask. I'd be happy to help."

"There is one more thing. I bought a bouquet of flowers today, hoping to give them to you. I'd hate for them to go to waste. Please take them with you. As a weak apology for missing our date."

"Please don't apologize. Consider everything taken care of, and keep me informed of your father's progress whenever you can."

"Thank you. We will be in touch soon."

"Please give my regards to Bette."

"Will do. G'bye for now."

Sad turn of events, to know that Bette and Jaimie's father was in a hospital thousands of miles away from his family. Of course, I was selfishly disappointed about the date, but as an unexpected twist, I found myself intrigued about his apartment. I never had the chance to tell Jaimie that I would be out of town. But that obviously had to wait. I decided to book my flight to Detroit for Monday afternoon. I hoped Abby could watch Poodles again.

Chapter 10

 *Washington, DC, 1933*

It was a formidable task, but Billy's art supplier suggested individual mirror tiles that, when meticulously assembled, looked like one large mirror. Hirsh was more than pleased. It was now up to Billy to etch his original drawing on the mirror. Billy dropped all responsibilities he had at the club except that one. He was the first one to arrive at the club each morning, and stayed until the lights were turned off. The etching took him five solid days and nights. On the sixth day, he told Hirsh he was adding the finishing touches. By day's end, the project would be complete.

That evening, Billy called Hirsh and Edward over to the mirror. Like any dramatic painting unveiling, Billy slowly uncovered the mirror. A few moments passed. Billy became concerned at the growing silence.

Finally, Hirsh spoke. "Son, that is a piece of art." He patted Billy on the back and still beaming, he added, "It looks exactly like the drawin'. Better if that's possible."

Billy looked at Edward, who managed, "Fine piece of work there, Billy." Edward wasn't as enthusiastic about the mirror, but if the boss was happy, well then he was happy too. Edward had never seen him this elated.

Calling, "Let's celebrate!" Hirsh ran up the stairs to his office and returned with a bottle of champagne. He found three champagne glasses behind the bar, popped the cork and poured champagne until it overflowed in each glass. "After all the problems we've had with construction and employees, our luck is finally turning around. I can feel it."

From the corner of the restaurant George watched the celebration with disgust. It was just a stupid mirror. What was all the fuss about?

Billy knew that Hirsh's response meant he'd become invaluable to Hirsh. He'd been a hard worker, reliable, never late, and always eager to please the boss. Seeing the mirror, Hirsh forgot all about the month's trial period. Billy was at the Mayflower Club to stay.

With the mirror in place, the first-floor restaurant was almost complete, and Hirsh turned his focus to the delivery of the gaming equipment to the building's third floor. Already in place, the deep red carpet gave the room a look of divine elegance. Dark wood wall paneling stretched from floor to ceiling. To the far right of the room, a long mahogany bar sported a gleaming gold rail. To the left of the bar was the closeted entrance to the gaming tables. Chandeliers glistened soft sparkling colors throughout the room. Each table was covered with fine white linen and an elegant, small silver tray that held a white candle and a red rose in a silver vase. The room was festive, yet refined.

There was one final plan still to implement, one last major detail—adding the gambling equipment to the back room.

The delivery itself took a week of planning. They had to study the police patrols, note the lengths of time between patrols, and note which patrolmen tended to nod off while on duty. Based on that spotty information, they scheduled the delivery between three and four a.m., in a disguised baked-goods delivery truck. It took several attempts—the patrol times unexpectedly changed, and some formerly lackadaisical patrolmen suddenly weren't as sleepy as usual—but on the fourth night's attempt they succeeded, and the equipment was placed in the back room behind the two well-concealed walls. The third floor was ready. Hirsh was ecstatic. And the liquor was being delivered in five days.

To work out any complications, Hirsh decided to open the restaurant a few days in advance of the liquor delivery. Besides, opening the restaurant first would more fully cement the club's main cover as a restaurant. He bought a quarter-page advertisement in the *Washington Post* to announce the opening of the restaurant. He scheduled the announcement to run after delivery of the liquor. By then they would have all the snags out of the restaurant's operation, and no sense in a huge crowd until the liquor was available.

On the day before the opening, Hirsh began to feel nervous. Not an unfamiliar feeling near inaugural day, but his stomach was in knots. And he needed cash. Between the renovation, workers, equipment, and now the food, there wasn't much money left. He wasn't rushing the opening, but was hoping for a few good profitable nights.

The employees knew about the booze and games on the third floor, but anyone who wanted to keep their job never discussed it. The third floor had a separate entrance and was considered a separate location. Even if a customer asked about liquor, no one acknowledged its existence. You just had to know that it was there. Word would spread soon enough. That was how it worked.

* * *

"When *ees* the food deliver?" Bruno, his head chef demanded in his near-indecipherable Italian accent. "I must know what I *ham serveeng*."

Hirsh had paid a lot of money to get Bruno. "I ordered everything you requested. Pheasant, beef fillets, lamb, oysters, shrimp patties, golden baby potatoes, spinach. It'll be here. You have plenty of time before tomorrow night. And get me the final menu. I need to get it printed."

"Final *meenu*! How can I put together final *meenu* without food in front of me?" Bruno huffed.

Why are chefs so temperamental? Hirsh thought. *For God's sake, it's just food!*

"Bruno, you're a master chef," Hirsh stated trying to boost the man's ego, as if it needed it. "I hired you to cook. I'll worry about the rest. The food will be here. Surely I'm not holding you up from finishin' the menu."

"Bruno not a miracle worker!" Bruno was flinging his arms in the air.

"The food will be here in a few hours. Get me the menu. We'll print as soon as possible. I'll open without a goddamn menu if I have to."

"Without a *meenu*! Impossible! I will have ready." Bruno brought his tone back to normal, but like an angry child, he stomped back to the kitchen. Hirsh didn't care. He knew the food would be excellent. So what if Bruno was eccentric. It was the least of his worries.

Hirsh looked around the restaurant. The dark mahogany wood floors matched the booths lining the walls. White tablecloths covered each table. Gold napkins, along with white plates trimmed in gold, adorned each table. Tiny lamps with small tassels provided a soft radiance. Fresh flowers in colors of deep red, white, and purple were abundant. Two majestic, eight-foot-tall palms lined the entrance. The mirror was prominently placed above the massive dark mahogany bar that, for now, served recently legalized 3.2 percent alcohol beer, along with fountain drinks, coffee, and tea. At least the choice of brew was better than with his previous club openings, thanks to FDR "modifying" the Volstead Act that very year. Nobody had wanted to buy near beer, and with only a half-percent alcohol content, Hirsh couldn't blame them. Sales of the three-two beer would be better, maybe enough to ease some of the pain from the liquor costs.

* * *

Hirsh continued to walk around the restaurant and, as he approached the stairs, he caught a glimpse of the mirror. Shaking his head, he paused at the ornate railing and said to Billy, "Son," he beamed, pointing at the mirror, "that is a work of beauty. I'll never get tired of looking at it."

Billy smiled. "Mr. Rosenburg, I hope you never do." As the artist spoke, he adjusted the crisp black bowtie of the tux Hirsh had fronted the money to buy. Another investment in having a successful opening. Details were everything.

* * *

Opening day for the restaurant arrived. The late-day sun provided a cast of shadows on the front entrance's parquet floor that sparkled in hues of gold and amber. Duesenbergs, Fords, and Bentleys arrived with men smartly dressed in their finest silk suits and women wearing the most updated Paris fashions from the Madeleine Vionnet collection. Times were hard, but the rich weren't as affected as the rest of the country. When the financial analysts began hinting that the stock market was growing too quickly and was due for a correction, many got out just before it completely collapsed, or had their money socked away in secret household wall safes. No one predicted the stock market crash would be as bad as it was, but by the time money began to leak from banks, many had their funds and gold bars safely stored away.

With the Depression still in full swing, a night on the town provided the wealthy and not so wealthy a distraction from the financial mess. The 1930s were the "The Golden Age of Fashion." A night out gave women an opportunity to shed their everyday-hausfrau clothes for something sparkly. By day the style was classic, *sweet*: tailored tweed with high collars in grays and dark blues, with matching plate-shaped hats. Evening dresses were different altogether. Women wore silk, calf-length chiffon dresses in colors of white, black, peach, and coral. The waist was accentuated with a crosscut design for a tight waist fit, highlighting a trim figure and long legs. Sequins and glass baubles adorned the dresses. They would be dressed to kill tonight.

* * *

The menus arrived on time. Adorned with a dark red tassel, they were printed on gold parchment paper and had a glossy smooth finish. Gazing at it, Hirsh decided that Chef

Bruno's well-planned, elaborate dinner menu would have suited a president.

"Boss, it's for you." Billy was holding up the phone.

Menu in hand, he hurried over. "Yes can I help ya?"

"Hello Mr. Rosenburg. This is Mrs. Butler. I called several weeks ago inquiring about an opening date? Do you have one yet?"

"Yes, ma'am."

"And when is that?"

Hirsh thought for a few seconds. He wanted to word this properly. "We will be fully open on Friday."

"Friday you say? I would like to reserve a table Friday night for six?"

"We aren't taking—"

"Look Mr. Rosenburg, I recommend that you take this reservation. I'd like to assure the party they have a guaranteed table. You will understand when they arrive. They also request a quiet table in a corner location."

"And what name would I be puttin' on the reservation?"

"Let's just use my name. In case you forgot, it's Mrs. Irene Butler."

Hirsh had nothing to write with. He repeated her name and then hung up the phone. Couldn't be the Feds, Hirsh thought. They were slicker, not that demanding. Hirsh was curious, but tonight's events cluttered his thoughts.

"Edward, come here and bring a pencil."

Hirsh took the pencil and as he wrote he said, "We have our first reservation."

Edward, pleased, asked, "When's it for?"

"Friday. Sounded official-like."

Hearing this took Edward's pleasure away. "Boss, you sure you want to be messin' with the government this early? We need to work out the particulars."

"I've opened, what, five clubs now? I know the particulars, as you call them. Friday. Make sure the third floor is ready."

Chapter 11

Los Angeles, 2015

Saturday morning was an early start. Since I'd be gone all next week, maybe longer depending on what we found, I needed to spend time at the office. I called Beverly and asked if she could meet me for a few hours.

I arrived to a stack of mail. Bev had gone through most of it, so at least it was an *organized* stack. There were checks to sign, deposits to review, correspondence to return, and a few personnel decisions to be made. I had to provide a quote for a new opportunity in Israel, and the job in Sydney needed my attention. It was a small site, but with time, I felt confident I could grow the business there.

After a few hours Beverly arrived. In moments, she'd ditched her purse in a desk drawer and sat across from me, iPad in hand, ready to take notes.

"Thanks for coming in on short notice," I said. "I won't keep you long."

"Welcome back. How long do I have you for?"

I couldn't help the smile. "That's one of the reasons I wanted to see you today. But I'll get to that in a minute. Remember Clarence Higgins?"

"The overdressed, sweaty guy? How could I forget?"

"He's hired us to take on a new project."

She lowered her chin but not her eyes. "And what country will you be jetting to now?"

"Fortunately, the one we're in. But it'll take me to Detroit, and possibly Washington, DC. He has some ... family problems that he'd like me to investigate."

She maintained the position, but if anything, the doubt in her expression grew. "So we're a detective agency now?"

"No, we are not. It's a long story. And I won't bore you with the details, but the project intrigues me, and I'd like to help."

"Lucrative, I hope."

"To be determined. Having said that, it very well could be. And quite frankly we could use some extra cash. Which is why I asked you here today."

She raised her chin and kept her eyes on mine. "Need me to jet off to a foreign country, meet with national dignitaries, and fall in love with a suave rascal who'll break my heart?"

"Wow. Where'd that come from?"

"I watched a James Bond movie last night. Guess it stuck."

"I never took you as a Bond girl."

A shrug. "Typically, I'm not. But it filled a void."

"Well, sorry to disappoint, but all the work involves this little office here." There was disappointment on her face. Maybe I could fix that in the future. "I need you to hire an assistant."

"For you? Are you firing me?"

"Good grief, no. Why would I want you to hire your own … never mind. An assistant for you. I can see that the workload here has picked up," I pointed to the stack, "and since I'm gone a lot, I'd like to know you have help."

"Don't you think I handle the load? Because if you—"

"You're misreading this. Or I'm a terrible communicator. Let me start again. I need a senior-type assistant. Not a partner, at least not yet, but an employee who thinks like a partner. If I have one criticism of you, it's that you're sensitive. I want you to start thinking of this as your business. Not just as an employee. I see potential in you and after the string of assistants who didn't get that, I have experience in this matter. Along with the title, you'll get a small raise. Not enough, but I need someone to help me grow this business."

She continued to listen. I thought I saw a vague smile. I needed to keep Beverly.

"And an annual bonus. Effective 365 days from today. But I need you to take on added responsibilities here. Sensitive information. Your resume and experience said you can handle that. Watching you work has proven your skills. So, I need you to hire a junior-type assistant who reports to you, not me. You deal with them. I tried to run this organization on a shoestring, and it cost me. Customers, new jobs. Who knows what else? I need someone to … Do you have a passport?"

"No."

"Get one. Apply this week. It takes four to six weeks to process. Then maybe I can send you to meet a dashing, heartbreaking cad, or whatever you called him. Seriously, I might need you to travel. Monday morning, passport office."

She nodded. "Mel, I know money is tight. I see the bills. But you're all I have right now. I need this job. I appreciate the vote of confidence."

"Good. I'm heading to Detroit on Monday. Probably gone all week. And maybe the next week. Call a temp agency. Get someone in here with an eye on hiring them full time. Let's start them at twenty hours a week, but make sure they're interested in full-time work."

"I've hired employees before. I can handle this."

With that out of the way, I handed Bev a short list of items I needed accomplished and sent her home. There was a wonderful sense of relief in this decision. Maybe I could save this little business after all.

I wrapped up the work as best I could. Before I left, I checked my texts for Jaimie's information; it was there. Curiosity took over so I decided it was time to visit his apartment. Besides, there were fresh flowers at stake; it wouldn't do to let them sit over the weekend.

I walked to the garage and opened the door to my old blue Beamer. As I started the engine, the same warning lights came on. Something about oil and an inspection. I'd been ignoring the lights for a while, hoping they'd just go away. I despised car maintenance. Maybe I'll deal the car when I get back.

I looked at the address that Jaimie sent to me and added to my GPS. Wilshire Blvd. Not that far from the office. The address turned out to be in a condominium complex. Très swanky from the outside. I found a place to park, which is never easy in Santa Monica, and entered the building. With the sound of my high heels loudly clicking on a cold granite floor, I, slightly embarrassed, walked toward a tall cherry wood desk.

"May I help you, Miss?" a security guard asked.

"Yes, thank you," I said, nervous, and when I'm nervous I tend to talk way too fast. "I'm a friend of Jaimie Wellford's and he asked me to pick up an envelope from his office," I rambled. "You see, he's out of town and—"

"Yes Ms. Danbury. Mr. Wellford said you would be visiting." They knew my name? "If I could just see some ID. I know it's inconvenient, but we ask all our visitors." Seemed a bit excessive, but I had nothing to hide although I felt like I did.

I placed my license on the big cherry desk and he took a good long look. I nervously tapped on the desk.

"Thank you very much. Here is the key to Mr. Wellford's apartment. Please bring it back with you after your visit." He looked in the direction of the guard that greeted me at the entrance. "Giorgio will escort you to the elevator. There is a phone on the thirty-fourth floor near the elevator. When you are finished, simply pick up the phone. It automatically rings the desk and we will send up the elevator."

"What if I want to take the stairs?" I had no idea why I asked this. I didn't intend to walk down thirty-four flights of stairs. Maybe it was my lack of finesse at following needless authority.

"You certainly may take the stairs. Our cameras will note your progress. If at any time you would like to use the elevator, simply use the phone located on every stairwell floor and we will direct you to the elevator. There is also a phone located at each elevator entrance."

Well that settled that. "I just asked in case there's a fire or I need an emergency exit."

"Of course, Ms. Danbury. You will find Mr. Wellford's home to your left as you exit the elevator."

I was sure this guy thought I was an idiot, but he did a good job of hiding the assessment. Giorgio escorted me to an elevator, placed a key in the slot next to a button marked "34th floor," and up I went. I exited the elevator and turned to the left, noticed the security camera watching my every move, and found my way to his apartment door. I pressed the code, turned the key, and unlocked the door.

I stepped onto a dark marble floor that led to a sunken living room. The ceilings must have been twenty feet high. Windows stretched from floor to ceiling and provided a breathtaking view of Los Angeles. Downtown buildings sparkled in the late afternoon sun. In the distance I could barely make out sailboats playfully bobbing about in a choppy Pacific Ocean. Reluctantly, I ripped myself away from the view and headed to the kitchen. With a hint of Mediterranean influence, the kitchen was painted in earth-tone hues, a matching, multicolor backsplash lining the back wall and distressed, raised-panel oak cabinets. I placed my purse on a massive cream-colored marble countertop that topped a huge kitchen island. Hanging in the center was the typical array of shiny copper pots and pans. On the counter, I noticed an arrangement of spring flowers. Being honest, I was a little disappointed they weren't roses. Too soon in our relationship for that. But they were indeed beautiful. I was taking them regardless.

I made my way through the living room and recognized two unmistakable Edward Wormley couches, accented with gold-tasseled pillows and matching cream-colored lounge chairs. Classic minimalist design with few accents. No family pictures or mementos anywhere to be seen. A gorgeous room, if with the feeling of a museum.

Jaimie hadn't said to take a tour of the place, but now that I was here, what was the harm? To the left of the living room were several doors. With one of the doors ajar, I saw what looked like an office in roughly the apartment's corner. Assuming cameras—if they were present, they weren't obvious—it was best to look professional just in case. I fought back the urge to peek into the master bedroom. That might've looked like I was some sort of creepy voyeur. Which I wasn't. I took just a few more minutes and walked toward the windows to again soak up the view, and then headed inside the office.

On the desk was a thick envelope marked "WB Final." Clearly, I should just take the envelope and the flowers and go. But I took a second to observe how everything was so neat and orderly. And sparsely appointed, similar to the rest of the apartment. Only a desk and a chair. That was it. Our home decorating choices couldn't be more diametrically opposed. The kitchen being the obvious exception. Relenting, I grabbed the envelope and as I turned to leave, a giant framed oil painting of a lion with piercing brown eyes gave me a startle.

My knowledge of art was not on par with my knowledge of furniture. I took a closer look. Most likely an original. I couldn't make out the name of the artist. I tried not to psychoanalyze the guy, but his apartment lacked any personal touches and the only picture hanging on a wall was of a super-scary intimidating lion. Before I put too much importance on that, I decided it was time to move on. I exited the office and took one last glance around the apartment, picked up the vase of flowers, closed the door, and walked toward the elevator. After picking up the phone—who was I kidding, I wasn't walking down thirty-four flights of stairs—the elevator quickly arrived.

Exiting the building, I realized that I'd never been to Warner Brothers. I'd done the Universal Studios tour, but had never been to the Warner Brothers lot. I could be as star struck as the next person. What if I ran into someone famous? It could happen.

* * *

On Monday morning I woke up early. Packed a suitcase in record time, hugged Poodles and Abby, grabbed Jaimie's envelope, and headed for Warner Brothers.

I arrived at the studio lot and without knowing what to do, drove up to the gate and told the guard that I was from Wangara Productions. The guard looked at his clipboard and to my amazement said, "Hello Ms. Danbury. Silvia Goldman is expecting you."

The nice guard gave me a pass for my car and directions to the office. The gate opened and as I drove to the office entrance, I tried to look casual, as though I visited movie studios every day, but found myself glancing every which way looking for someone, anyone famous. I arrived at her office, no star in sight.

I opened the door to a large reception area. The receptionist greeted me with a firm handshake and asked if I would mind waiting a few minutes. "Of course not," I said, and hoped I didn't sound like an overeager bumpkin.

I settled into one of the plush, overstuffed couches and looked around. Tranquil spa music played quietly in the background. The furniture was a shiny, polished mahogany wood. Definitely not Ikea. Walls were accented with deep red and tan-color paint. Pillows of the same colors scattered about. Nice office for Miss Sylvia I thought and decided to google her name later. After a minute or maybe two, the professional mannered receptionist directed me to Sylvia's office.

"Thank you so much for bringing the proposal. I understand that Jaimie had a family emergency. Hope everything is all right?" Sylvia said this almost as if she was prying.

"I hope so too," I said without giving specifics. I couldn't help but notice that Sylvia was strikingly beautiful. Tall, trim, long blond hair neatly and professionally clipped back. Perfect makeup, and she was wearing a signature red couture dress.

"Please give my love to dear Jaimie," she said.

Dear Jaimie? Give my love? I wasn't liking what I was hearing.

"Of course I will." I managed to sound genuine, I thought.

I gave her the package and thanked her, and while walking out the door, I still had hopes of running into someone, anyone famous. I hopped into my car, and slowly drove to the exit. Again, no star in sight.

Driving to the airport, I reflected on this interesting day. How life can change when new people enter your world.

Chapter 12

 Washington, DC, 1933

The first few nights went off without a hitch. Only the restaurant was open, but the food was exquisite, the service impeccable, and customers left with promises to return. Hirsh could not have been more pleased.

The second night, after all the patrons had left, LeBeck's delivered the liquor through the hidden back entrance. Delivery of the booze was as tricky as the gaming equipment. In the past his distributors resorted to using laundry vans or trucks. Opening a restaurant made linen delivery a good cover. On a few past occasions, Hirsh would have the liquor delivered in broad daylight. Bold, but in the neighborhoods the last clubs were situated, it worked. Not an option on a street like Connecticut Avenue. The "bread truck" arrived in the early morning hours, as scheduled.

Edward and George unloaded the liquor without drawing any attention.

They worked all Thursday night on the third floor, setting up the liquor and putting finishing touches on the card tables. The door in the back of the building, which only allowed entrance to the third floor, had a tiny opening for passwords. There were two guards at this door, one on the second floor and one at the entrance to the third floor. Any one of the guards were authorized to usher a guest out before they entered the speakeasy. These well-trained gangster types didn't come cheap, but Hirsh was glad to pay them well.

The third night brought the first monkey wrench in the crankshaft. More than one. "Bruno, I smell something burning!" Hirsh bellowed. "What is that smell?"

"*Eef*'s one of the new ovens. We fix right away!"

Hirsh watched Bruno scurry back into the kitchen and heard him yell at anyone and everyone in sight.

With a satisfied nod, Hirsh walked to the front window. Rain poured down, just like that first day waiting for the realtor. He didn't believe in superstitious hooey, but, as he gazed out the window, he had a creeping, ominous feeling. Just then the sky lit up as a bolt of lightning illuminated passersby dodging raindrops for safer ground. Hirsh had seen enough to shake him; he turned around and walked toward the bar.

"Where are the goddamn flowers?" he shouted toward Edward.

"Billy's pickin' them up right now, boss."

"We open in three hours. Three *hours*. The kitchen's on fire, there's no flowers, and where's the menus?"

Edward stepped closer so he could speak without shouting. "Boss, the kitchen ain't on fire. Bruno is handlin' it. Menus are underneath the bar. Antonio is finishin' the tables, and the flowers will be here any minute. Let Antonio and me worry about this."

In a huff, Hirsh replied, "I'm heading upstairs. Come get me when you've fixed this mess."

No point in responding, so Edward didn't say a word, just watched Hirsh march up the stairs, thankful he was out of the way.

* * *

Word was out about the third floor. Subtly placed invitations to select clientele had been made. At seven p.m. exactly on that Friday night, a shiny gold Duesenberg arrived and the party of six emerged at the restaurant's entrance. Hirsh had made a point to be available, greeted the party, and recognized Senator Martin Hughes immediately. A six-term senator in this town didn't go unnoticed, yet Hirsh knew not to address him by name.

"Welcome to the Mayflower Club. I'm Hirsh Rosenburg, the proprietor."

"I'm Mr. Sullivan," one of the men in the party announced. "We have a reservation under the name of Mrs. Irene Butler for six."

"Right this way," Hirsh snapped his fingers and his senior waiter appeared. "This is Antonio. He will be taking care of you this evening. Please call upon me if I can provide any additional service." Antonio greeted the guests with a polite bow and showed them to their table.

There was a glow about the restaurant. The afternoon thunderstorm left the air cleansed; the entrance had been shined and polished, and dusk-bringing sun cascaded through the front windows. On the second floor, the setting sun's rays casted the mirror in dramatic fashion. The comments from Hirsh's guests were all similar: "Where did you get such a lovely mirror? Who is the artist?" It was the highlight of the restaurant, as Hirsh knew it would be.

The senator and his guests ordered a leisurely dinner, and as their Baked Alaska arrived Mr. Sullivan left the table and approached Hirsh.

"And how has the evening been so far, Mr. Sullivan? I hope to everyone's satisfaction?" Hirsh said politely.

"Mr. Rosenburg, I'm sure my guests were pleased with the dinner service. I am curious, sir, about a place we can go to extend the evening?"

"There is a place I can recommend. Exit this building, turn to the right, then right again, and ask for Mr. C. That's all you need to do. I will see to it that the enjoyment continues."

Mr. Sullivan went back to the table and whispered in Senator Hughes's ear.

Hirsh spoke with Antonio briefly, and then took the concealed elevator to the third floor. It was ten-thirty p.m., and the joint was already lively. Customers gathered around the bar, ordering rounds of drinks, buying liquor by the bottle and swaggering back to their tables. Men in three-piece suits gathered in small circles, discussing the recently signed New Deal's Federal Securities Act, the massacre in Kansas City by Pretty Boy Floyd, and the first Major League Baseball All-Star Game. In the back room, the roulette table spun. The card tables were full. Cigar smoke invaded the air.

Hirsh had hired hookers too, from a local whorehouse he'd used for his past clubs. His cut was small but keeping his clientele happy was worth the extra money.

Senator Hughes and his entourage entered the club. It was apparent that the senator was familiar with speakeasies. He ordered a Canadian Club on the rocks. The ladies ordered the finest champagne, and the party continued.

In one corner of the room a six-piece band played jazz, and the place was jumping. Edward kept a lookout near the front window, and with guards on every floor, Hirsh's jitters began to fade.

Hirsh noticed Oscar entering the club with a bleached-blond bombshell young enough to be his granddaughter. Hirsh knew this wasn't Oscar's missus because he'd met Oscar's homely wife at a previous club.

"Oscar, my friend. Welcome to the Mayflower!" Hirsh beamed with enthusiasm.

"I see you're finally open," Oscar said with a gleam of riches in his eyes. "Doll," he reached into his wallet and pulled out a hundred-dollar bill, "get me a whiskey and yourself a bottle of champagne. Tonight, we celebrate the good fortune of my dear friend Hirsh." He patted Hirsh on the back.

"Yes, Oscar baby," she smiled at Oscar and walked away happy to be rid of him.

"Hirsh, my old pal, you've done it again," Oscar took a cigarette from his silver case, gave it few good taps, and Hirsh lit it for him.

"Yeah, and I had to pay a fortune this time. But I intend on makin' a shitload of money."

"I'm countin' on it. I'm not here to discuss our arrangement. You got a square deal from me." That was open to interpretation, but Hirsh was in too good a mood to contradict Oscar.

"You put the tables in the back room?" Oscar said through a billow of smoke.

"Yeah. The one with the side exit. I don't expect no trouble, but it's an easy out."

Hirsh walked Oscar to the gaming area. The tables were full.

"Any tables I should stay clear of?" Oscar asked.

Hirsh knew what he meant, but he never rigged any of his tables, although he'd been accused of such, numerous times. He never felt it was worth it, and rarely took a financial bath. Whiskey and whores were all he needed to guarantee loose tables. His stance had not proved him wrong.

"You know that's not how I operate, Oscar," he replied.

"Thought I'd check to be sure."

At about two a.m., the evening ended without incident. Finally, money was pouring in. Hirsh knew the senator would be back, and hoped he would spread the gospel to the DC, faithful. The evening could not have gone better, and this thought carried him all the way to his office, where he sat behind his desk. Buoyed by how well the night went he took off his shoes and, rubbing his aching feet, was still smiling when Edward entered the office.

"That's the last of the dough from the bar upstairs, boss." Edward placed gold coins and large bills on the desk.

Hirsh looked at the pile of cash, not needing to touch it to know that his first night's take was more than he expected. After counting the bills and the few gold pieces, he looked up at Edward. "Most goes in the safe. Take the rest and put it where we discussed. Keep a ledger of where stuff goes so we know what we got. I'll set aside Oscar's dough from this pile." He was nodding at the cash for the safe.

"Got it, boss."

They parted at the stairs. Edward headed upstairs to the third floor, making sure the doors that led to the gambling area were locked and secure. Hirsh walked down the stairs but stopped at the bottom step when he saw Millie sitting at the bar. "I'm pooped," Millie said as he walked over to her. "Are you almost finished? I want to go home."

"Darlin', I'm almost done. You were superb tonight." He gave her a peck on the cheek and ignored her pout. Any rotten mood that his wife might be in wouldn't spoil the night for him.

While Edward locked up the club and, even when he walked out of the front entrance, he thought he saw the same two Feds he'd seen a few weeks before. But he couldn't be sure. Let them hang around all they want. He wasn't worried.

Chapter 13

 *Detroit, 2015*

Before I left for Detroit, I sent Jaimie a text about my success in delivering the proposal. I inquired about his dad. I didn't hear back before my flight. Not sure if that was a good or bad sign.

I tried to remember if I'd ever been to Detroit and I couldn't answer for sure; the downside of a life of travel means that destinations become muddled. Maybe the airport would jog my memory. I had booked a room at the Hilton downtown and rented a car. Clarence offered to pick me up at the airport, but I was more comfortable driving. I didn't consider myself a control freak, but who considers themselves anything negative in life?

After arriving in Detroit, I called Clarence and got his voicemail. I'd never received his voicemail before, and hesitated about leaving a message. I decided that not leaving a message was best; he'd still see my number. There was no message from Jaimie either. No sense in questioning whether he got my text. I'd let it go, for now.

I checked into my room and tried Clarence again. This time he answered.

"Hello Miss Mel. I take it that you arrived safely?"

"I'm here," I said, though I was sure I sounded a bit weary. "When would you like to meet?" No pleasantries needed. It was late and I hoped he'd say tomorrow.

"I'll meet you tomorrow at the house." He rattled off the address. "Thank you for coming, Miss Mel. I'm anxious to get started."

I put the phone down and started to unpack. Walking back toward the bed, I saw my phone's message light blinking.

"Hello Melinda. I received your text. I can't thank you enough for helping me with the Warner Brothers proposal. I didn't have time to warn you about my building's security. It's rather tight. I assure you it's not for me. There must be someone famous or infamous in my building. Dad is better. Still very sick." He paused for a moment. "Not out of the woods, which means I'll be here for at least another few days." Another pause. "Well that's all from here. Thanks again and hope you liked the flowers. G'bye for now."

Was it wrong to hope for a little more? Like he missed me, or couldn't wait to see me, or couldn't stop thinking about me? Okay, that last thought might've been a stretch. We'd only just met. And after all, the man was dealing with a sick father. No wonder I was still single. Selfish to the end.

* * *

Tuesday morning I arrived ahead of schedule, and parked out front of a modest three-story house on a street lined with houses that looked transplanted from the 1960s. Clean, well-maintained homes, but the entire neighborhood had a dated look. As I made my way up the brick front steps, I noticed two old rockers on the front porch and a few potted plants that could use a little water. I rang the doorbell and a young woman answered the door.

"Hello. Is Clarence at home?" I peeked inside.

"You must be Miss Mel. I'm Sara. My granddaddy is around here somewhere." She opened the door and I stepped inside. It occurred to me at that moment that I'd never asked about Clarence's family. Or that I knew next to nothing about him.

I looked around the house while I waited for him. The house had old wood floors that creaked when you walked on them. There was a front main living room and a parlor to the right. I could see a kitchen in the back and a set of stairs leading to ... what was it ... two more floors? Several of the windows were stained glass. The sun cascaded their colors onto the wood floor. Simply beautiful. There wasn't much furniture, but the house was up for sale so I didn't expect to see much in the way of decor.

Clarence walked into the room and I heard the floor creak with every step. He wiped his hands on a towel before he shook mine. "Sorry, Miss Mel, that I wasn't at the front door to greet you. Sara here made breakfast and it was mighty good." He looked at Sara and gave her a wink. "Are you hungry? Cause there's plenty left."

"It does smell marvelous. But I ate at the hotel. You must be quite a cook, Sara."

"Granddaddy was just hungry. It ain't all that good. Anyway, nice to meet you Miss Mel."

"Sara, could you bring two glasses of tea, dear?"

"Yes, Granddaddy."

He looked my way. "It's sweet tea, Miss Mel. It's the only way we know how to make it 'round here."

"That's fine. When in Rome ..."

"When in Rome, what?"

"It's just a silly saying." I changed the subject. "Your house is wonderful. Are you set on selling it?"

The tea arrived.

"Yes, Miss Mel. I believe I must. It needs a lot of work and I don't have the money to fix it up proper. The better investment right now is frankly ... you. I ain't tryin' to put any pressure on you, but I know I got somethin' here. I'm more convinced ever' day."

I worked well under pressure, but the thought of this guy giving me his life savings made me nervous. The less I knew about the money, the better I'd sleep. I moved on. "Let's start with a tour of the house, shall we?"

"Of course. Where are my manners?"

Tea glasses in hand, we walked toward the kitchen.

The kitchen floor was a mix of black and white tiles. The cabinets were old-style white metal cabinets, and there was a light-green stove and matching refrigerator. Somehow it worked.

"There's little cookin' going on in here unless Sara's around," he said. "Her mom, my daughter Janice, did not inherit any cookin' skills. She's downright bad at it. We keep it as a secret."

Sara missed the humor he intended. "It ain't no secret, Granddaddy. She's a horrible cook and everybody knows it."

He glanced to make sure I was holding back my smile, as he was, and continued. "Well, I don't tell no one. Except I guess I just told you. Anyway, this is the kitchen." We walked back through the living area and up the stairs. The second floor had two bedrooms, which we breezed through, and then Clarence took me to the third floor. I remembered he called this a bedroom, but it was more of a loft. He pointed toward the loose floorboards and briefly mentioned the suspicious guy he caught nosing around the room.

We walked to a dresser that had seen its share of paint and Clarence picked up a nondescript metal box. He opened the box and pulled out a drawing. I'd seen my share of building schematics, and I instantly recognized it.

"Any ideas what this is for?" I asked.

"Well, I ain't exactly sure, and this may sound crazy, but the layout's nearly the same as the old Mayflower Club in Washington, DC. I think I mentioned before, my uncle worked there with a man named Hirsh Rosenburg."

I nodded. "What else is in the box?"

"Look at the bottom there. See the rust?" I did. "Looks like a small key was there at one point. Probably the key to a box. Key isn't there now. Which makes me suspicious about the flooring guy. I thought I saw him put something in his pocket that might've had the color of metal, but I couldn't be sure. I don't know what else he might've grabbed. There's also a picture of the club as it was back then."

"What was it called now? The club, I mean. I forgot."

"Dirty Martini. Building looks the same. I took the drawing in the box to the place. That's how I know it matches the floor plan of the club. At least of the main floor. And look at the drawing of a box in the corner. Looks like the box is behind a wall? And this picture that was taken inside the club? See the big mirror on the wall? What could that be? Somehow it looks like the box is below the mirror."

"I see that. Rather cryptic. Did you notice anything else when you were at the club?"

"Not really. I was thinkin' about talking to the manager or the owner, but what would I say? They wouldn't believe me anyway. Some old guy saying there might be money hidden in the club. Didn't want to give them any ideas either."

"Probably wise to keep it to yourself."

"I also found a record book. Numbers that don't make sense to me."

He showed me the book. It was actually a ledger, old style, like an accounting ledger.

"These look like dollar figures," I said. "And these letters—'A,' 'G,' 'O,' with dates. Don't know what this means." I felt like I had more questions than I did answers. Clarence was not deterred.

"I know what you're thinkin'. I was confused too. Still am. Don't give up on this Miss Mel. Too much here to be nothing. We have an appointment with Hirsh's granddaughter, Dorothy, tomorrow. Like I told you she's in a rest home, and as far as I can tell, she doesn't get any company. I asked the staff and they ain't seen no one but me visitin'. She has her wits about her, and for bein' eighty-six, she looks to be in great health. She wouldn't say nothing to me but goodbye. My uncle used to say her parents, Cecilia and George, were awful. Her momma was a drunk and her daddy was abusive. She knows somethin', Miss Mel. I just know it. I can't get her to talk."

I couldn't pull my gaze from the drawing, but I listened to every word. "Well, I hope she sheds some light on this. And I'm not deterred. There's enough here to keep us going. Anything else in the house that might help us out?" I looked at him.

Clarence and I stood at the dresser. He opened up a drawer and pulled out a piece of old paper, a drawing of road lines and a cross. A very rough drawing, but I thought it might be a map.

"This was in the box too. I can't make out the writing, but it looks like some kind of map of a cemetery. See the box with the cross on it? Looks like a coffin. And see there?" Clarence was pointing to a spot on the drawing.

"What is that? A tree?"

"I haven't been to the cemetery. So I don't know for sure. But it's like my uncle was trying to mark the location for some reason. Miss Mel, he told me that Hirsh's granddaughter Dottie, goes by Dorothy now, knew where the money was. He said he tried to find her, but as soon as the Mayflower Club closed down, Dorothy and her mother left town."

"What happened to the father? George was it? Maybe he has the money? He worked at the club, right?"

"That's part of what I can't find out either. I haven't been able to find any record of him anywhere. And Dorothy—"

"Won't discuss him."

Clarence nodded. "Edward insisted that George didn't have the money, so I guess we should start with believin' that."

The sheet was yellowed and hard to make out. "That isn't much help either. But if it was in that box, maybe it was something the guy planned to take until you showed up and stopped him. Maybe it'll make sense at some point. What time are we meeting Hirsh's granddaughter?"

"I'll pick you up at ten o'clock tomorrow. The retirement home is about thirty minutes from here. Miss Mel, I do appreciate you being here. I hope I'm not wasting your time."

I gave him a smile I hoped would reassure him. "Clarence, this is a challenge. I won't lie. Maybe it's what I need right now. There are a lot of missing pieces here. Let's see if I can … encourage Dorothy to talk. And we'll take it from there."

We walked down the stairs. I said goodbye to Sara and decided to head to my hotel to spend some quality time on the internet.

Chapter 14

 Washington, DC, 1933

The club had been open only a few months, yet word of the third floor had spread. Its reputation kept the tables booked on a nightly basis. Between the food, booze, and gambling, Hirsh had never been more successful. On weekends, the club was packed with politicians, movie stars, and DC,'s wealthy, drinking and gambling until the wee morning hours. News continued to swirl around repealing the 18th Amendment, though all restrictions remained in place. Even with the eminent legalization of liquor, the Feds were still a problem. Or perhaps the Feds, sensing that their control over alcoholic spirits was soon to end, decided on a last gasp of harsh surveillance and punishment before their fun was no more. Hirsh continued the security measures at each entrance to the club. Liquor from LeBeck's was transported in the early morning hours. The separation between restaurant employees and club employees remained in effect. No one discussed the gambling room. It remained by invitation only.

Though always valuable to him, Billy was becoming indispensable to Hirsh. He was a smart kid who waited tables, worked in the kitchen, and had even begun working behind the bar on the third floor when the third floor became busier, faster than Hirsh expected.

"Billy, I need you to go to LeBeck's and see about more whiskey," Hirsh said after one particularly busy night. "I can't have us runnin' out. We have two big parties this weekend and I know I ain't got enough."

Hirsh wrote down the quantity he needed. "I don't care what kind. I can always bottle-swap." When inventory got low on the good stuff, Hirsh would add the lower-cost whiskey to the bottles. He didn't like doing this, but it was only occasionally and when absolutely necessary.

"Pete knows you're comin'." He handed over the paper. "Leave about midnight."

"Yes boss. Anything else I should be gettin'?"

"Grab a few cases of champagne. I didn't ask for it but he should have some lyin' around."

The club was quiet that night, and at about twelve thirty Billy took the truck to LeBeck's. Bootleggers kept odd hours, he mused while driving. They were usually open between ten at night and seven the next morning. This was Billy's first trip alone to LeBeck's, though he'd been with Hirsh several times. He didn't expect any trouble. Traffic was relatively light. Billy occasionally glanced in the rear view mirror to make sure he wasn't being followed. He never noticed the tail.

Billy pulled up to LeBeck's. Following Hirsh's routine, he parked near the building, where he could see the entrance but not be noticed, and waited a few minutes. An occasional car rolled by, but nothing looked suspicious. He started the truck and parked at the side of the building, got out of the truck, and walked up to an old brown door, and knocked. He gave the password, took one last look around, and walked inside the building.

LeBeck greeted him and pointed to the alcohol stacked up in the corner.

"Hirsh asked for three cases of champagne too," Billy said.

"I got it."

The two men who'd pulled up after Billy went inside, sat in their car and watched as the liquor was loaded into the truck.

Billy drove back to the Mayflower Club, unmindful of the same car driving two or three cars behind. He pulled up to the back entrance and unloaded the booze, then parked the truck and headed for the third floor.

"Any trouble?" Hirsh questioned when he saw him.

"Nope, and I was able to pick up the champagne."

"Good work."

Billy liked pleasing the boss. He knew that Edward was Hirsh's partner, but had plans on changing that someday.

* * *

On a semiweekly basis, Edward continued to supply Oscar with a share of the take. In the beginning, Oscar questioned the amount of his share. But as the weeks rolled by and the amount substantially increased, Oscar became less belligerent. Why wouldn't he? This was easy money for Oscar. The reward far outweighed his risk. The club was surpassing even Oscar's expectations. But just the same, he liked to keep Edward in line.

"You're late, Eddie," Oscar grumbled during one payoff. Edward hated being called Eddie.

"Boss had me runnin' errands." Edward saw no reason to elaborate. "It's all there. This week's take."

"There better not come the day when I have to question ya. Wouldn't end well for you, Eddie," he said with a sneer. "Hirsh trusts you, but I don't. Never did trust no Negro, 'specially with money. Don't you ever hold out on me, boy."

Edward had heard all this before. He shrugged and replied, "No suh. You can call Hirsh to check."

"I may just do that."

Edward knew Oscar was too lazy to call anybody. He'd hoped these unnecessary trips to Oscar's office would soon end. Maybe Hirsh could eventually trust Billy enough to let him be the runner. Edward thought about putting a bug in Hirsh's ear.

Oscar's office was within walking distance of the club. Edward didn't like walking late at night with cash in his pocket, but he never took a driving exam to get a driver's license. Oh, he could handle a car, license or not, but preferred not to.

He opened the door to the club, and as he turned the corner and entered the main restaurant, he saw Billy carrying a familiar box upstairs. Billy must have gone to LeBeck's alone to pick up more liquor. He knew that Hirsh never left the club at night without one of them being there. He also knew that Billy had never driven to LeBeck's by himself.

He waited until Billy walked back down the stairs, and asked him, "Did you pick up booze at LeBeck's?"

"Yeah, the boss asked me to make a run."

"Any trouble?"

"None that I saw. I did what Hirsh said. There wasn't much traffic, and I was only at LeBeck's for a few minutes."

Edward only shook his head, satisfied by the answer. But he had an uneasy feeling about LeBeck's. He couldn't trust anyone anymore. Or maybe he was thinking too much. One thing he was sure of: he wanted out of this line of work.

Chapter 15

 *Detroit, 2015*

I was downstairs promptly at ten, and Clarence greeted me in the lobby.

"Good morning, Miss Mel. I hope you had a pleasant evening."

"I did, Clarence. But to be honest I didn't sleep well. I spent several hours on the internet researching the Mayflower Club. Didn't find much. I'll need to leave after our meeting today and get to the public library in Washington. No doubt local newspapers will have more information about a speakeasy that was around in the thirties. I'd also like to see the location where the Mayflower Club was located. Dirty Martini, I think you called it." Which sounded like a place I wanted to be right now.

"Well, I have hot coffee in the car waiting for you. Won't help get you to DC, any faster, but maybe that'll help with thinkin'."

Hot coffee it would be. I briefed Clarence on the information I did find, which confirmed that the club was a speakeasy and a fancy one at that. Catered to the wealthy, including many politicians. "Looked like it opened in the summer of 1933. The year will help in researching the club." Between sips of the best coffee I'd had in a long time, I explained that the library would be my first stop in Washington. "And of course I'll stop in at the restaurant, to check the place out. And maybe have a cocktail or two."

The laughter we shared carried over into the drive to see Dorothy, until we arrived at her retirement home, Fountain View. I'd expected an old, institutional-looking nursing home. If the exterior was any indication, I was wrong, wrong, wrong. "On a scale of 1 to 10," I whispered to Clarence while we headed up the walk, "this place is a 10."

We entered the lobby and I noticed a set of antique but perfectly preserved Victorian chairs and a long, matching, ornate crimson sofa with cherry wood trim. The lighting, provided by cherry wood floor lamps, was subdued. A tranquil entrance, probably by design. We were greeted by a young woman seated behind a massive desk that resembled a bar. More like a swanky hotel check-in counter than a receptionist's spot. Adding to the ambiance, a wall fountain quietly bubbled next to the desk.

"May I assist you today?" she asked.

"Yes, thank you," Clarence replied. "We are here to see Dorothy Clemmons."

Carol, whose name I'd read on the placard, glanced at her computer screen. "Oh, yes. You must be Clarence Higgins and Melinda Danbury. Can I see some identification please?"

We provided our ID to Carol and after typing for a few long minutes, she returned the cards to the top of the desk.

"Please have a seat and we'll direct you to the visitor's area shortly."

Clarence and I settled into the comfy plush sofa, and I couldn't help but comment, "This is a nursing home? I almost thought we were at the wrong place."

"It is extraordinary," he replied in a low voice. "Wait until you see the visitor area."

That reminded me of something I should have already done: set our roles for the upcoming session with Dorothy. "Let me do most of the talking," I whispered. "See what I can find out. Maybe, since I've never met her before, I might have some luck. Or it could go the other way too, I suppose."

A few minutes passed and an elderly gentleman in a three-piece suit walked toward us. Clarence and I stood to greet him.

"Hello, I am Fredrick Wiltshelm. I understand you are friends of Mrs. Clemmons?" His German accent was heavy but understandable.

We introduced ourselves and Fredrick continued. "Mrs. Clemmons is expecting you. If you will please follow me."

We were pleased to follow Fredrick through the lobby, and entered a door that led to what must have been the visiting area. As we entered the room, I noticed a small kitchen on the right. Fresh fruit, pastries, coffee, and a silver tea service were displayed on a glistening black countertop.

Fredrick asked if we would like some refreshments. Clarence politely said no. I could've used another cup of coffee, but I declined too. Swiveling my neck to stretch it from the drive, my eyes fell on a small camera near the ceiling. If Fredrick noticed my recognition of it, he didn't let on.

I'd thought the large, yet cozy room, was where we'd meet Dorothy, but we moved on. Fredrick led us down a short hall into one of the smaller private rooms we passed on the way. No cameras here that I could see, just two couches, a few chairs and a rather plain, yet well-polished cherry wood table. Clarence and I glanced at each other after Fredrick left but waited in silence for Dorothy to arrive.

The door opened and Fredrick escorted a strikingly beautiful old woman into the room. Her navy dress was saved from dourness by being expertly tailored to show off a slender figure, and helped along by a multicolored scarf and a necklace of small but genuine-looking white pearls with earrings to match. Her light-gray hair was pulled back into a loose bun. A few intentional curls framed her cheekbones and slender neck, emphasizing makeup perfectly and freshly applied. She walked with a cane yet carried herself with *Vogue*-like glamour into the room, and I couldn't help but wonder if she'd been a dancer when younger. *Clarence said she's eighty-six? That seems imposs—*

Startled to see that he'd already risen to his feet, I bolted from the couch, definitely lacking dancer form, and joined him in introductions.

"Mrs. Clemmons, I will be right outside should you require my assistance," Fredrick said after he helped her into one of the chairs, placing her cane handle over the chair arm within easy reach.

My initial awe of her had subsided, and I decided to get right to the questions. Besides, based on Clarence's frosty reception before, I had the feeling that further pleasantries wouldn't be well received.

"Mrs. Clemmons, thank you for taking time to visit with us today. Clarence and I have been looking forward to meeting with you to discuss some dealings of your grandfather's."

Maybe that was too rushed. Or too blatant. Dorothy's response was to look at me, and then at Clarence. Whoever said silence is golden, was mistaken. With no option otherwise, I waited out the uncomfortable silence.

She stayed quiet. I did too. Until I'd waited long enough.

"Before I go any further, let me make sure you're aware of the arrangement that Clarence and I have. I'm an archeologist. I run a small company called Danbury Archeology." I hurriedly dug out my card and placed it on the table. "Clarence came to see me three or so weeks ago, asking me to assist in finding, shall we say, some family possessions. Typically archeologists search buildings, caves, that sort of thing, looking for clues and treasures linked to the past. Clarence is hoping that my experience in locating … valued objects, might help with his search. I thought it was a bit of a stretch at first, but have come to the realization that the two—"

Dorothy finally spoke. "I am well aware of what an archeologist is, Miss Danbury, and I know why Clarence hired you. He thinks there's money hidden somewhere," she glared at Clarence. "I can assure you, I know nothing about any money hidden or otherwise."

No sense in giving credence to her just yet. I continued on as if I didn't hear her denial.

"Let me tell you what I know from discussions with Clarence and from my limited research on the internet. I understand that your father, George, and your grandfather, Mr. Rosenburg, were employed at the Mayflower Club in Washington, DC, in the 1930s. Am I correct so far?"

Dorothy simply nodded in agreement.

"Good. Okay. The Mayflower Club was a restaurant and also a speakeasy that undeniably offered gambling and liquor, both illegal at the time. I am not condemning your father, Mrs. Clemmons. Prohibition was just about over in 1933, and alcohol was in practically every establishment in some form or another. But according to Clarence, his Uncle Edward did mention that a good amount of money was lost or stolen. Did you ever talk to your father about this?"

"Yes. And I told Clarence this too. My daddy died when I was young, and after his death my mother and I lived in Detroit. In those days, who knew what a lot of money was. Honestly, I don't know what all this fuss is about. Let me repeat myself. I don't know anything about money or a missing key."

I didn't mention a key. I decided to try a different angle. "Do you have any other siblings?"

"No. I have no other family." She looked at Clarence and directed her next words to him. "You're wasting your time. I told you this last time you were here. If there is any money, I have no idea where it is. Why would I? I was a child back then."

"I understand." Actually, I didn't, but she wasn't budging.

"Miss Dorothy," Clarence chimed in, "my uncle and your dad worked at the club. Every time I was around Uncle Edward, I never had the impression that he was anything but sincere about the money. Even if it did seem somewhat unbelievable. He thought your dad stole money that rightfully belonged to my Uncle Edward. He said he earned it while working at the club, and it was substantial. The hard part was believing he was a partner in the business. I never gave it much thought, but the box we found had a picture …"

Trying to keep Dorothy from noticing, I placed two fingertips on his knee. Best he not give too much information, at least not yet.

"What box?" Dorothy asked.

Clarence realized he'd said too much, but knew he had to answer to keep her from clamming up. "I found this old box with some strange documents. I can't make heads or tails of it, but it mentions the Mayflower Club and something about money. Nothing that I could understand, though, ma'am."

I hoped she bought this explanation. She seemed to. I changed the subject to the room's lovely décor, and both of them seemed relieved. After a few exchanges about Victoriana, I decided it was time to leave.

"Well we certainly appreciate your time today, Mrs. Clemmons. I have just one last question. Have you ever been to Washington, DC?"

"I have. We lived there while daddy worked at the club."

"I'm sorry. I meant have you been in recent years?"

"I know what you're thinking. I have visited as a tourist like most folk. But I've never been to the Mayflower Club or whatever it's called now."

The Mayflower Club 138

"I love Washington, DC, myself. You would be surprised at how many people haven't taken the time to see our nation's capital," I said, trying to find some comradery.

"Well, that is a shame."

Clarence and I stood. "We don't want to tire you. You have my card. If you can think of anything that might be noteworthy, please call me, or Clarence. By the way, this is a beautiful place."

"It is nice." Dorothy became a bit more agitated. She didn't sound convincing.

We opened the door and I noticed that Fredrick was literally guarding it. Convenient.

"Thank you again," I said to Dorothy, and Fredrick escorted us to the front desk. "Would it be possible to have that cup of coffee?" I asked him.

"Of course," Fredrick replied without any sign of agitation. "Cream and sugar?"

"Just cream, thank you. Clarence?"

None for him, thank you, but I wished he'd said yes to maybe delay Fredrick's return. I needed a few more minutes to look at the lobby without being conspicuous.

My expression casual, I glanced around and noted there were two cameras in the lobby. Lots of spying for an old folks' home.

My coffee arrived. I thanked Fredrick, and we exited the building. As we stepped outside, Clarence asked, "Well, what do you think?"

I sipped while we walked. "I never mentioned any keys. How'd she know about a key? She knows more than she's telling us. And I didn't get the impression she liked it there. Did you?"

"I don't know what to think. But she was certainly agitated about somethin' besides me. Or you. And I don't recall ever mentioning a missing key to her either."

"Did you notice all the cameras in the place? What's that about?"

He drew off his hat, rubbed his gray hair, and placed the hat back on his head. "I can't say I did. They are everywhere these days, maybe in nursing homes too?"

"Everywhere, true, but that many? Seemed excessive to me. Especially in the lobby. Do they expect a jail break from a bunch of old people?"

I took one more glance at the building as we got into the car. "Yeah. Nice place. What was her husband like?"

"They divorced when I was young. So I can't say. She never remarried as far as I know."

"They never had any children, I take it."

"No, they never did."

"Where did she live?"

"Near us, in a similar neighborhood."

"Did she have a job?"

"As far as I know, she was a clerk at the local grocery store."

Not quite *Vogue* material when young, then. "A grocery clerk, huh … If that was her only income, then where'd she get the money to afford this place?" I asked as we drove off.

Neither of us had an answer that did anything but create more questions.

Chapter 16

 *Washington, DC, 1933*

It was a sultry Thursday night and the club was jumpin'. The hookers were scantily dressed, all looking for a paying date for the night, and the jazz band was just heating up. Bourbon was being sold by the bottle and card tables were full of inebriated gamblers happily losing their hard-earned cash. The restaurant was filled to capacity with customers dining on $25 pheasant and Steak au Poivre. As a finishing touch, waiters were scurrying to and fro carrying gleaming silver platters filled with double chocolate cake and strawberry parfait. Money was flowing on every floor.

It started to go sideways at about eleven thirty.

Jimmy, the first security guard, opened up the peep door for passwords. All he saw were badges.

"Open up, son. This is a raid conducted by your United States Treasury Department," came a voice through the tiny opening. "We have reason to believe you are in violation of the Volstead Act."

Jimmy snapped to the next security guard, Frankie, "Get Hirsh, now! Tell him to clear the joint!"

Frankie ran upstairs, past the second-floor guard, and burst through the door to the third floor. "It's a raid. It's a raid! Everyone out. Now!"

Hirsh turned around but didn't need to see the expression on Frankie's face. Everyone knew the drill. Most of the people present had been through raids before. His first task was corralling the patrons, and they were scattering everywhere. Hirsh called for Billy, and he and Billy led them to the two sets of staircases that would take them to the back street. Once downstairs, they'd all be on their own.

Every guard was well trained to stall the cops as long as possible. The second-floor guard made each agent show their badges through the peephole, one by one, and only then did he ease open the door. Impatiently, the cops broke through the door and made their way to the third floor. The third-floor guard followed the same procedure, stalling as much as he could, but it only took a few minutes for the cops to make it to the bar area.

It didn't matter. By the time they got through the door, the place had emptied. As soon as the raid was announced, Hirsh had quickly closed the door to the gaming area and then closed a front door he'd designed to look like a plain wall. Once certain that Billy had the patrons on their way out, Hirsh made his way out the back third-floor entrance and reentered the restaurant. He sat at the bar and waited.

All the employees in the bar area had been instructed to leave too. They'd gone over this before. No sense in anyone getting arrested and more importantly, saying too much. There was a paddy wagon parked out front holding a few people, but most customers had exited the back entrances and got away. The diners in the restaurant remained. There was no booze in the restaurant and, legitimately, they weren't part of the raid.

Minutes rolled by until Detectives McCarthy and Mahoney appeared. They'd walked back down the stairs, out the back entrance, and into the restaurant through the front door.

They saw Hirsh sitting at the restaurant bar, talking to a customer. McCarthy strode his way, Mahoney following. "Look Mr. Rosenburg, you ain't foolin' no one," McCarthy said. "We know there's booze up there. You can smell it everywhere. But my question to you is, where's the games?"

"Would you please excuse me for a minute?" Hirsh was speaking to the customer. "Apparently the detective here needs my attention." The customer gave him a confused smile but picked up his soda and left for a table, where he immediately started a round of whispering among the other diners.

Hirsh looked at McCarthy with an indignant expression. "Look, Detective? ..."

"Detective McCarthy."

"Detective McCarthy, we had a private party going on upstairs. That's all. There was a small amount of booze. Hardly enough to get anybody drunk. And you searched the premises, I assume. I don't have any gaming equipment. That's illegal, you know."

"Don't be a wiseass. We know what's going on here. We'll find it. Maybe not on this trip. But I know your type. You'll be opening back up soon enough. It won't take long. I'm not wasting my time taking you downtown for bullshit booze violations." He took his billy club and pointed it in Hirsh's face. "I'll be patient and wait for the big payoff. Trash like you don't wait long afore you're back in business. Good luck cleaning up," he pointed up, toward the third floor. "Seems you have messy guests."

Detective McCarthy took his time ambling around a mostly silent restaurant. "If any of yous know about gambling going on here, kindly let me know. We won't take you in."

He waited for a full minute, and no one moved or spoke.

Hirsh watched the detectives walk around the restaurant, trying to intimidate his customers. They walked up to several tables and barked out questions and veiled accusations. Still no one said a word.

The detectives made their way back to the front of the restaurant, glared at Hirsh in disgust, and exited. Hirsh let out a sigh of relief.

After the paddy wagon left, the remaining diners quickly finished their meals and exited. Within minutes, only employees were left in the restaurant. By this time Edward was downstairs. In a raid, Edward was responsible for the employee count. At any given time, he could tell Hirsh how many employees were in the bar and restaurant area.

"All accounted for, boss. No one was pinched, nobody ran off."

"How about the guards?"

"We're good there too."

"Well that's somethin' at least. We've been so careful. How the hell did they know about the back entrance?"

"Look, boss, we're lucky they didn't find the games. You know what I'm going to ask ya, and I know what you're going to say. So I'll save my breath. We had plenty of warning this time and they didn't seem to notice the elevator here in the restaurant, but all they need to do is plant someone and we're—"

"Fucked. I got it." Hirsh paused speaking, his angry tone mounting. "Have you noticed that most of our customers work for the government? Do you think I like schmoozing with those idiots?" He was now yelling in Edward's face. "Insurance, Edward! Insurance is why I laugh at the senator's stuffy jokes, why I look the other way when they bring their cheap whores, why I buy the best booze in town. You can't do it, Edward. You can't schmooze them. They not talking to you! Billy's too young and George is a halfwit! It's me that keeps this place open. No help from anyone here." As Hirsh said this, he raised his arm and pointed around the restaurant. And with that, he walked up the stairs and back to his office, and they all collectively shook as they heard the office door slam.

The room was quiet. After a few uncomfortable minutes, Edward, always the peacekeeper, said, "C'mon Billy. Let's see what the third floor looks like."

Chapter 17

 *Detroit, 2015*

After our visit with Dorothy, I went back to my hotel to catch up on some work. My plan was to head to Washington tomorrow. I finally had a chance to look at my phone and noticed a few missed calls. The first return was to Abby, to check in. All was good at home, she said. My mother called just to find out where I might be. I really should call more often. After my father died, Mom decided to move into a senior living community not far from where I lived. I told myself she was fulfilled with new friends, bowling, cooking, and other activities. But really, I had no idea. Maybe I should plan to visit when I returned. Whenever that was. This proclamation made me feel better. No call from Jaimie. But it had only been a day.

As I put my phone down, it started ringing.

"Miss Mel, Miss Mel, he's here! What do I do?" Clarence. Panicked.

"Who's here?" I said with forced calm, hoping calm transmitted through the cell towers.

"That guy. That floorin' guy. He's outside. He's tryin' to look like he's just hangin' out there, but I know it's him. He thinks I'm not here. I'll bet he tries to break in."

"Okay. First, thing to do is calm down. Don't do anything unless you think you're in danger. I'm only a few minutes away. I'll be right there." I hung up, grabbed my purse, and made for the door. To do what, I wasn't sure.

It took less than fifteen minutes to reach Clarence's street. I thought it wise to drive down the street and pass by his house before I made any decisions. I'd learned that Clarence could sometimes exaggerate situations. As I whizzed by his house on the right, I casually glanced over and saw a man in a parked car. I kept driving. He appeared not to notice me. I continued down the street and hit Clarence's number on my cell.

I turned the corner and noticed a narrow alley behind his house. "Meet me behind your house. Let's see if we can get this guy to leave and then follow him." I thought a moment. "Right before you leave, turn on a light. That'll tell him someone's home. Maybe that'll get him to leave."

"Okay, Miss Mel," he whispered. Not sure why he was whispering, but I let that go. I pulled around the back of his house into the alley. Clarence bolted out the back door.

As he closed the car door he said, "I turned a light on. Let's drive around and see if he's still there." Clarence was unnerved now. I was too and needed to stay that way.

We pulled out of the alley and turned onto the street. The car hadn't moved. I pulled just past the entrance to his street and turned the car around, then stopped next to a big bush that obscured my car but would allow me to see the back of flooring guy's car. "Let's wait him out," I said with the confidence of a true detective.

It didn't take long. Within minutes, the car began to pull out. Not being a boyfriend stalker by nature, I couldn't remember ever following anyone before. I tried to remember what I might have read in a book, or maybe seen by a real, acting detective on TV. No tips came to mind. But Clarence was moving restlessly in the passenger seat, and I needed to remain calm. Or at least act like I knew what I was doing. I waited just seconds and then started to follow.

"Do you know what you're doing?" Clarence asked.

Did I accidently say something out loud?

"This is easy," I said and dismissed the thought with a brush of my hand. "I doubt he suspects anyone's following him, which gives us the upper hand." This I did believe.

We stayed several cars behind. Clarence knew the streets so we took minor detours along the way. We drove for about twenty minutes, and it appeared the guy was clueless about our tail.

He turned down a dirt road. With no streetlights. I hesitated.

"Do you know where this road leads?" I asked Clarence.

His voice sheepish, he said, "I lost track of where we were a few miles back."

Not the answer I'd hoped for, but I decided to follow the guy. I waited a moment more and turned down the same road.

He didn't drive too far before he turned into a long unpaved driveway leading to a house. No way to follow him now without being spotted. I heard a car door slam and we watched him go inside.

Clarence looked over at me. "What do we do now?"

I looked around to see what was nearby. "Let's come back later tonight. Maybe he'll go out again. If he leaves, maybe we can poke around the house for the key or other clues."

"What if he doesn't live alone?"

A possibility I hadn't considered. "If we come back and it looks like there are too many obstacles, I'll think of something else. But we need to find what evidence he has, if any. And we need that key."

We drove back to Clarence's house in unsettled silence. It dawned on me that I'd asked an elderly, nervous man to help me break into a house. "Clarence, I don't need you to go with me tonight. I'll be okay and believe me, I won't do anything crazy. I'm just gonna poke around a bit."

"Oh no you don't. I'm not excited about goin' back. But you ain't goin' back alone. I'm coming with you— Hey, I might know someone who can help us. A friend 'a mine, let's say more of a business acquaintance, that knows a thing or two about breaking and entering."

My eyebrows rose under their own power. "Care to elaborate?"

"No. But this guy knows his stuff, and for reasons I'll not go into right now, I trust him."

Driving back to Clarence's we decided to meet back at ten p.m. That was a few hours away. On my way to the hotel, I wondered what a burglar should wear. Something dark. I didn't bring any break-in clothes with me to Detroit, so I decided to detour to the nearest mall and buy a few things. Good thing I was thinking this through.

At ten on the dot, I pulled up to Clarence's house in black Ralph Lauren pants and Under Armor shirt. Thought I might as well buy clothes I'd wear again. Although the shirt was questionable. Abby might like it.

Clarence must have seen me pull up; he and the "breaking and entering" acquaintance immediately headed to my car. Clarence got into the front seat.

"Miss Mel, this is Hank."

I looked in the back seat. Hank, or whatever his real name was, was a strapping thirtysomething.

"Nice to meet you, Hank," I said, not sure what else to say to someone who probably wanted to keep identities obscured.

No comment. I rambled on. "I brought coffee and sandwiches, in case we're in for a long night." It's what they did on TV.

I tend to talk too much in uncomfortable situations, and when my kind offer was also met with silence, I found myself asking Hank too many questions. Not prying, just making conversation. More than once, I looked at him in the rearview mirror, but his eyes were always on the window. After a while I realized he wasn't going to suddenly engage in conversation. It was probably best to stop talking. Or try to. The silence grated at me, so I started again, but stuck to the case.

"Did Clarence tell you we're looking for a key?"

Hank simply nodded. Silent, but at least it was a reaction.

"Good. Let's find the key and grab anything marked with the Mayflower Club, Fountain View, or the name Dorothy Clemmons."

"Good thinkin', Miss Mel. There might be other stuff in there linking him to this," Clarence stated with confidence. He looked back at Hank. "If it's in there Hank'll find it."

No nods this time; Hank had returned to window watching. Hopefully he had some experience finding things in houses. Not too different from my profession, although mine was legal.

"Hank, I feel better that you're along," I said. "Hopefully this won't take too long."

"Clarence likes you, Miss Mel. I help out my friends."

Just in time, I bit back my gasp. "Well, I want to help Clarence, too." We had that in common.

We arrived at the street and I turned my headlights off. We looked down the road, didn't see any cars, and no lights showed from the house.

"What do you think?" Clarence looked in Hank's direction.

"I say we hike to the house. Get a closer look. Too risky taking the car down there. Let's park the car toward the street in case we need to make a run for it."

Although I didn't like hearing, "make a run for it," the rest of his idea was sound. I parked the car within a small cluster of houses I'd seen just before the street. It was a short walk through a dense field to the house. Plenty of areas to hide, I reassured myself. Hank had a few handy tools with him: a flashlight, small walkie-talkie radios. Not too different from what I carried on a dig. But there was one thing I didn't: a souped-up lock-picking kit. I also noted he had a gun. It never occurred to me that we would need guns. I decided to leave that thought to myself. Hank wasn't the type to agitate with unimportant questions from novice burglars.

"Here's what I'm thinking," Hank said to us. "Clarence, you stay outside." He handed him one of the radios. "Press that button if you need to reach me. Don't say anything. Just press the button. I'll know that means it's time for us to get outside. Mel and I will go inside and grab any keys we find. Can you describe the key at all?"

"I never saw the key, but it was small," Clarence said. "Like it fit into a box. Not a house key. The pattern needs to match the stain in the box."

We should've brought the box, but too late now.

Hank couldn't read my mind, so he only nodded. "Mel will bring out what we find and if we have time, you look through them. If we don't have time, we'll take them all. Figure it out later."

I looked at Clarence and we shared nods.

As we approached the house, we looked around and waited a few minutes to make sure no one was home. We opened the back fence, still no lights or activity. Hank whispered to Clarence to stay by the fence and keep a look out. He instructed one more time about radio silence unless absolutely necessary. We both shook our heads up and down. So we weren't real burglars, I thought, but we understood the instructions.

We walked up three back stairs and Hank took out a tool. We were in the house in seconds. Hank paused for a moment, listening. Nothing to hear. He handed me a radio and softly said, "Let's work rooms together, but if we separate and you have to reach me, then use the radio, just like I showed him." I bobbed my head again in agreement. Hank was calm. I was a bundle of nerves.

We started in the kitchen. I found a key chain with keys and gingerly grabbed it, trying to keep the keys from jingling. Hank looked through drawers and found a couple of loose keys. They didn't look small, but I took these outside to Clarence just to be sure.

I returned to the house and didn't see Hank. I decided to follow the instructions and not use the radio. He couldn't be far. I worked the living room. There were some papers on a table. I riffled through them. Nothing mentioning the club or Dorothy, but wait … an invoice from Fountain View? I grabbed that. Seeing no keys anywhere, I left the living room and peeked in the bathroom. Nothing unexpected there. There was no place left to look on the first floor. I decided to head upstairs.

On the way up, I heard footsteps. Had to be Hank. As I reached the top of the stairs, I heard what sounded like a commotion. I had no idea what to do. Should I run? Should I check out where the sound was coming from, or just freeze in a panic like I was doing now? The third option was useless. As I walked toward the sound I heard, "Get the fuck out of my house, you motherfucker!" And I saw Hank, through the open door, as he punched a much smaller man in the stomach and then hit him with an uppercut to the jaw. The guy fell to the floor, bleeding. He looked up at Hank, who had covered his face with a mask since I'd last seen him.

I didn't have a mask—didn't think of one at the mall—but from where I was standing, I didn't think the man could see me. Hank gave the guy one more blow to the head, and the guy stopped moving. Then he raced toward me and said in a voice that sounded too calm, "Got to go. Now."

We raced down the stairs and out the back door. Clarence's face showed confusion, then surprise when Hank grabbed his arm and started pulling him along. We ran as best we could with Clarence; the poor guy was wheezing, and I hoped he wouldn't die on us. We made it to the car, and none of us could have missed the flashlight, coming from the woods. We all jumped into the car.

Hank saw my panicked look and calmly stated, "Start the car."

I obeyed, threw it in gear, and we squealed away. I saw the flashlight's beam shining in the car, but thought we were too far away for any good description. It might have been the guy Hank beat up, but that seemed unlikely, since last I'd seen him, he'd been unconscious.

"What happened?" Clarence looked in my direction.

"Ran into some trouble," Hank answered. "Short guy, came after me. I took care of it. Thought he was out cold, but pretty sure that was him with the flashlight."

"Jim is a tall, skinny guy, and he has some sort of tattoo on the back of his neck. I couldn't see in the dark, but the man with the flashlight didn't look like Jim," Clarence said. He must have seen that confused look on my face. "The flooring guy said his name was Jim," Clarence explained.

"Oh."

"Well, that weren't Jim then," Hank acknowledged.

"How'd he get in the house?" I questioned. "I don't think he was there when we arrived."

"I walked around the back of the house for just a minute. Thought I heard something. He must have pulled up while I was back there," Clarence admitted. "This is my fault. As soon as I saw the car, I mashed the button."

"Nothing happened. It's okay," Hank, the man of few words, said.

"Any luck with the key?" Clarence asked as almost an afterthought.

Hank fished through his pocket. "This it?" There was no traffic. I turned on the overhead and fixed my gaze on the rearview mirror. He held up a small, rusted, black key. Squinting, I made out a small 's' on it.

"Why Hank, yes, I believe it is," Clarence said with a smile on his face.

I chimed in on my successful find. "I found what looks like an invoice with Fountain View's name on it. Ties him to the place."

"Let me see that," Clarence said.

One hand on the wheel, I handed the document to Clarence, but seeing headlights coming our way I snapped off the overhead; it made us conspicuous.

He turned on the flashlight and looked at the document. "Looks like an invoice for fifteen hundred dollars. That's a lot of money. Wonder what he does for that place? It has to be tied to Dorothy."

"Don't lose that, Clarence. Might be able to use it later …" It sunk into my head that Clarence was most likely in danger now. "Clarence, I can almost guarantee that whoever that was will be contacting Jim, if he hasn't already. And Jim knows where you live. You can't stay at your house. We can stop for a few minutes while you grab a few things. You also need to call your daughter and tell her and your granddaughter to stay away."

"My daughter lives in Indiana. Janice and Sara were just visiting. Not worried about them." Clarence thought for a moment. "I guess I could get a hotel."

Clarence wasn't grasping the situation. "Let me be more specific. You can't stay here in Detroit." I let that sink in while I devised another plan. "Why don't you come with me to Washington? You can help me with research at the library and we'll check out the club together."

Silence. Then, "Miss Mel, I'm living at the house until it's fixed up and I can sell it. If I leave it empty … what if there's a fire, or a break-in? I can't live in Washington, DC."

"It's not permanent," I clarified. "It's just until we get more of the story. But you need to stay *waaay* clear of the house until we understand what Jim and his crew are up to."

"What about Hank?" Clarence asked.

I looked at Hank in the rearview mirror.

"That guy don't know me. I got to stay in Detroit." Hank spoke to me but kept his gaze fixed on Clarence. I didn't ask why because I didn't care, and frankly, considering his conversational skills, the thought of him coming to Washington with us wasn't thrilling for me.

"And the woman is right," Hank added. "You need to stay away from the house."

Not thrilled about being called "the woman," either, but I was glad Hank agreed with me.

"Hank, you should stay away from the house too. But maybe you can help us by checking on it every once in a while. I'm thinking that Jim or someone close to him might be back. Just stay out of trouble."

"I can do that."

We arrived at Clarence's house, and he went inside to pack for a last-minute trip to America's capital.

There was silence in the car, and though I thought he might bolt, Hank made no attempt to leave. Once again, the tense silence.

"Listen Hank, you probably saved my life in there. I thank you for coming along tonight. I mean it. Thank you."

"Miss Mel, it's what I do. You need me in Washington, DC, or anywhere else, Clarence has my number." And with that, Hank opened the door, looked my way, and got out of my car. He didn't drive off immediately, but waited for Clarence to join me. As we drove off, Hank started his car and drove off in the opposite direction. Even some criminals have a decent side, I thought. I hoped he would be okay.

Chapter 18

 *Washington, DC, 1933*

Hirsh sat at his desk and tried to calm down. Sitting still was not going to change the situation. He called Millie and told her about the night's events. She said she would drive over to see what she could do. Hirsh hung up the phone and took the elevator to the third floor.

He entered the room and saw smashed bottles and glass scattered everywhere. Dishes, "coffee" cups, and whiskey bottles thrown around like paper confetti. The cops even smashed two of the chandeliers. Several wood panels were damaged and would have to be replaced, and the carpet was torn in spots. He could see where the cops tried to pry open parts of the wall looking for the gaming gear. At least that held up, he thought.

As he looked around the room, he wondered how many more times he could go through this. Assholes. And there was nothing he could do but fix the place up as quick as possible. He knew the Feds wouldn't be back until they could confirm the location of the card tables. With luck, they never would. All club employees knew there was a gaming area, yet only a few people knew how to find it. Hirsh thought about the private party scheduled for Saturday night. He had to get the club in reasonable shape by then. The night's take was too big to miss.

After Millie arrived, she followed Hirsh around, patting him on the shoulder, saying it would be all right. That didn't help. Billy, George, and Edward walked around looking like they had no idea where to start. Hirsh yelled directions, and they gathered all the garbage cans, placed them in the center of the room and began picking up the trash. Millie, drink in hand, would pick up one piece of glass, walk to the trashcan, throw it in, and then pick up one more.

At the rate they were moving, cleanup alone would take until Saturday. But it was now three a.m., and everyone was exhausted. With Hirsh's okay, Billy went to his sister's house for sewing supplies. A seamstress, she followed Billy back to the club to see what she could do.

Edward began to take down the damaged panels. They had a few spare panels, but not enough to replace all the damaged ones. He'd have to find a carpenter in the morning to replace what he could.

George continued to pick up some of the glass that was strewn about, but after a short while he returned to form, went downstairs, and fell asleep in one of the booths in the restaurant.

At five a.m., Millie told Hirsh she wanted to go home. Hirsh sent her on her way and then returned to his office and fell asleep. He awoke to a knock on the door.

"Sorry to wake you, boss," Edward said, realizing he sounded as weary as he felt. "I'm heading out to get some lumber. I know Billy picked up more booze, but do we need to get any? We got that big party comin' on Saturday—"

"I'll check inventory. Who's left at the club?"

"Billy's here with his sister. She's fixin' the carpet, and George is asleep somewhere."

"Okay. Hurry back. We got a lot to do."

"Yes boss."

Edward closed the door. Hirsh got up from his desk, readjusted his suspenders, ran his fingers through his hair, and went to check on the liquor inventory. As a rule, he kept the supply at the bar to a minimum, with strict guidelines for his bartenders. When the bar supply was down to two bottles of certain brands, the bartender would notify Edward, and more would be supplied.

Hirsh reasoned the Feds couldn't have destroyed too much. The remaining liquor was well hidden on the second floor. He knew they didn't find it, or he'd be in jail right now. Few knew the exact location of the booze. Hirsh was still grateful for the supply Billy picked up just the night before. It might get tight, but they should be okay.

After checking the inventory, Hirsh confirmed he had enough for Saturday night's party. Word typically got out about a raid, and he figured the crowd would be down for the next few days until memories would begin to fade. No sense in risking a drive to LeBeck's for more.

On his search for the lumber and paint, Edward knew there were usually a few starving carpenters hanging around the lumberyard looking for work. With their help, he felt confident he could repair the damage before the club opened. He started to think about what Hirsh had said to him after the raid. He'd seen Hirsh angry before, but rarely was it directed at him. Something had changed with Hirsh. He knew he was wasting time trying to figure out. But it bothered him just the same.

"Have a nice night?" Detective McCarthy said as he walked in step with Edward. Detective Mahoney was on his other side.

"Whaddaya want?" Edward replied with his head down.

"We know there's tables in there. Care to tell us where to look?"

"I don't know what you talkin' 'bout," Edward said, still trying to ignore them.

"We're fairly sure you do. It might be wise to tell us. I'd hate to see your mug behind bars."

"I ain't in any trouble, and don't plan on bein'."

"Then the smart money is on cooperating with us."

"I got nothin' to say."

"Think about it. And by the way, tell your friend to be more careful when he's buyin' liquor. We needed him to deliver the booze to the club to prove the Volstead Act. Next time we'll arrest his ass."

The detectives stopped walking and Edward continued on, toward the lumberyard. But their words stayed right in front of his mind.

So they'd followed Billy. Edward wasn't surprised or concerned. The Feds knew about the booze. They needed probable cause to raid the club. Billy gave them that. No sense in letting Hirsh know. Billy was a good kid. He'd watch him a bit closer.

He fought it, but the wooziness was getting too hard to ignore. With the morning's heat and the intense fatigue, and now this confrontation with the Feds, he wasn't thinking clearly. If he were, he would have realized that their liquor distributor was exposed now too.

Chapter 19

 Washington, DC, 2015

After Clarence and I landed in DC, and checked into our hotel, I decided a drink was in order. I asked Clarence if he'd like to join me for a trip to the old Mayflower Club. Clarence claimed exhaustion and he'd been there before, and decided to stay at the hotel.

The restaurant was close by and it was a sultry evening. I took the opportunity to walk to the restaurant. As I passed DuPont Circle and ambled down Connecticut Avenue, I noticed the restaurant on the left, across the street. I stopped and tried to envision how the four-story building would've looked in the 1930s. Above the entrance was a black awning with the restaurant's name emblazoned on each side. There were tables outside, and I noticed there were two entrances, not one. One entrance to the first-floor restaurant, and a door on the side that must lead upstairs. I decided to write down the details so I wouldn't forget later.

I walked inside the restaurant and a friendly waiter escorted me to a table. Above a long bar to my left was a large mirror. Engraved on its surface was an image of a scantily dressed girl sitting in a martini glass. In one hand she held a stirring stick that resembled a stripper pole, and in the other hand a martini glass. When I moved to the right, then the left, her eyes seemed to follow me. The restaurant had a staircase to the right that led to an upstairs balcony, and I wondered if that accounted for the second outside entrance.

Bar-height tables paralleled the bar and booths surrounded the perimeter. The crowd was light, which meant I could look around if I wanted without being obvious. A different waiter asked what I'd like to drink. I asked for a recommendation; he suggested a vodka martini. "Perfect," I said.

While waiting for my drink, I decided to take a walk up to the balcony. The stairs looked like they were made of mahogany. They made creaking sounds with each step, and looked slightly worn though in excellent condition. I wondered if these were the original stairs. As I stepped to the top of the stairs, I looked out to the floor below. The mirror was the focal point of the entire top floor. There were tables and chairs for dining and as I looked over them I noticed a hallway to the right. While I began to wonder where that led, out of the corner of my eye, I noticed a man walking toward me.

"Can I help you?" the good-looking guy said.

"I'm sorry. Is it okay that I'm up here? Such a beautiful restaurant, I wanted to take a look around."

"Of course. Of course it's fine. Let me introduce myself. I'm Jack. I'm the evening manager. Is this your first time here?"

"Why yes it is. And I can't help but admire the mirror. Where did that come from?"

"You know, I'm not sure. This club dates back to the thirties, and the mirror's a replica of the original mirror. We only know that because there's a picture of it in an old newspaper clipping. I believe one of the prior owners had it made. We really aren't sure. It's become a trademark of ours."

"How long has this been the Dirty Martini?"

"We've had the restaurant for five years. It's a tough business, the restaurant business, and the owner bought it out of bankruptcy. I know the crowd's light now, but if you stay until ten thirty or so the place will be packed. We have a dance area and a hookah bar that's popular with the kids. Of course by kids, I mean twenty-to-thirtysomethings."

"I understand. Just out of curiosity, are there any records from back in the thirties? I'm a bit of a history buff."

"No. I'm afraid not. When we took the place over, it was cleaned out. Not a piece of paper anywhere. All we know about the place comes from stories people have shared with us. Apparently, this was a speakeasy back in the day. I'm sure there's information on the internet as well, but I haven't taken the time to look." I followed his glance to the first floor; sure enough, the light crowd wasn't quite as light anymore.

"Please look around," he said. "And if you're a history buff, have one of the waiters show you the hidden elevator."

He gave me a raised-eyebrow smile. "Who knows what nefarious activity it led to?"

"Thank you. I just might. And thanks for your time. I'm sure there's a vodka martini downstairs with my name on it."

"Anytime. I recommend the salmon for dinner. It's a favorite."

Jack bowed slightly in my direction and returned to wherever he came from. I took my phone from my purse, snapped a few pictures, and returned to my table downstairs. A third-floor elevator? The archeologist in me wanted to know more about that. But first, a drink.

Either the martini was fantastic or I was overdue for alcohol. I decided to take Jack's recommendation for dinner. While I waited, I couldn't help noticing that the crowd had picked up. A young crowd, which reminded me I wasn't anymore. I leisurely ate a delightful dinner and after another martini, or was it two, I asked my waiter about the elevator. "Come with me," he said. I almost thought he anticipated my question, but that was silly.

He took me to the front of the restaurant and indicated a spot behind a wall. My eyes were drawn to a door I couldn't have seen without his direction, which wouldn't be easily found unless one knew about it. He opened the door, and I saw it led to the elevator entrance. There were no visible buttons. To my inquiring look he opened a latch and pulled a switch, and the door opened. A small elevator. Padded walls sporting three buttons to the second and third floors. I began to feel claustrophobic as the elevator slowly creaked its way to the third floor.

"My, this is an old elevator," I said. I didn't see the typical "call for help" phone that elevators I knew had. I hoped I wasn't outwardly sweating.

As if he read my mind he said, "It sounds old, but it's inspected regularly. I'll bet there's a lot of history in this old elevator." I was sure he was correct in that statement.

We finally reached the third floor and he used a hidden lever to open the door. When we emerged I learned that, once again, the elevator was behind a door that led to a small room. We passed through that room into what looked like a disco, complete with a DJ playing loud electro dance music and flashing lights all around us. Now I knew I was old; this was slightly irritating. The waiter took me to the back and then outside, to the hookah bar.

"What are they smoking?" I yelled in the waiter's ear.

"It's a combination of flavor and steam. Tobacco's illegal, so we provide all kinds of flavors."

"I don't get it. What's the point?"

"You know, I'm not sure. But it's popular."

As I looked around, I noticed windows on what must have been the fourth floor. "What's up there?" I asked.

"Nothing really. Offices and some storage."

We left the hookah and dance areas and went down a different set of stairs to the outside.

"There are lots of entrances and exits to this building," I noted to the waiter.

"I think most speakeasies designed their buildings that way. I'm still not sure we know all of them in this building." He winked my way.

Making our way back to the front entrance, I noticed an alleyway that appeared to be located behind the bar area of the restaurant. Upon a quick peek, it looked like a narrow alcove with a dead end. I made another mental note.

I thanked the waiter for his time. Jack greeted us at the entrance. "How was your tour?" he asked.

"Fascinating. You have a real piece of history here. Thank you so much for letting me look around."

Jack said, "We hope to see you back again sometime."

"You can count on it," I said. "I'd come back for the vodka martini alone."

He escorted me to the entrance. "Have a nice evening."

I crossed the street and took a last look at the building at night, then turned and walked back to DuPont Circle on my way to the hotel.

Chapter 20

 Washington, DC, 1933

It took more than thirty-six hours, but by six o'clock on Saturday, the third floor of the Mayflower Club had been cleaned up. There were a few remaining scars. The color of the wood stain on the new panels was ever so slightly different from the color of the existing panels. The carpet was sewn to cover the most noticeable tears, tables were moved to cover the worst damage, and Billy was able to find two smaller chandeliers to replace the ones the Feds had knocked down. It wasn't a perfect match to the others, but the difference was hardly noticeable, and they looked as though they'd been the originals.

The raid wouldn't make the newspapers until Sunday. Hirsh wasn't worried about losing the party scheduled for Saturday night. A wealthy lobbyist, and more important, a regular client, was hosting a post-wedding party. His daughter was to be married in St. Agnes Catholic Church and after a two-hour-long wedding mass and a reception full of Anti-Saloon League teetotalers, Floyd Guthrie was going to be ready to cut loose. Floyd was too busy on Saturday to hear about the raid, but even if he did know, Hirsh knew he wouldn't cancel.

* * *

After Floyd sent his daughter and her new husband off on their month-long honeymoon, he drove his wife home and said he had some business to attend to at his office. He'd been a most gracious host at the wedding and even took a few days off before the event to help with last-minute details. But Washington, DC, never slept and he must get to the office to attend to the important business of the People. Floyd's wife always understood. That's why he loved her so much.

Floyd and his entourage arrived at the Mayflower Club at ten thirty. Hirsh personally greeted Floyd and all his guests. Hirsh had asked Edward to keep an eye on Floyd, knowing the man wasn't only a boozehound, but also used cocaine. Methamphetamine had been introduced in the 1930s and for the most part supplanted cocaine, but Floyd was hooked on the white powder. Heroin was always available, and Floyd took that on occasion too. Few knew of Floyd's drug habits. Hirsh was well aware. He'd been around cokeheads on many occasions as a bar owner and always recognized the signs. Although Hirsh was a drinker, he never touched drugs. He rarely drank during business hours and would only do so when clients demanded it.

Floyd was in rare form. His girlfriend, Mitzy, had been hitting the powder too. No matter to Hirsh. Floyd's guests were spending a lot of money gambling, drinking, and dancing. By all accounts, the party was a hit. At about two-thirty a.m., Edward lost track of Floyd. By that time, most of the guests had left. Mitzy left with a wealthy younger man and from all appearances, Floyd couldn't have cared less. Hirsh was busy speaking to a few of the remaining guests and was unaware that Floyd had gone missing.

After spending several minutes searching the third floor, Edward found Floyd in the restaurant, passed out in one of the booths. He tried to awaken him, but couldn't. Then he took in Floyd's pale and clammy skin. When he couldn't tell if the man was breathing, in a panic, Edward took the elevator to the third floor, found Hirsh, and whispered in his ear.

"Would you kindly excuse me?" Hirsh said to the guests, "Edward has brought to my attention a matter that I must attend to."

Hirsh and Edward took the elevator back to the first floor, and Edward pointed toward Floyd. Hirsh rushed over and was relieved to find he was breathing after all, but each breath was labored. He felt for a pulse. Present, though weak. Hirsh knew he had to get him to a hospital, but after the raid, there was no way he could take the chance and call a doctor or an ambulance to come to the club.

"Whada we do boss?" Edward said beside him.

"Shit," Hirsh shook his head. "We gotta get him to a doctor. Find Billy and get him down here. He's too green to close the place on his own. Take the receipts. Lock them in the safe in the office. I gotta stop by LeBeck's tonight and pay for the extra liquor Billy picked up. Can't risk pissin' him off. Go get fifteen hundred from the safe. That should cover any money I owe LeBeck and if I need a bribe on the way."

Edward did as instructed, then found Billy and brought down the money. It took all three of them to carry Floyd to Hirsh's truck.

"You locked up the money from tonight?" Hirsh asked.

"Yes boss."

"Okay. Finish cleanin' up and go home. I'll call you on the telephone if somethin' comes up."

"Yes boss. Don't worry 'bout nothin'. Just be careful. Billy, keep an eye."

Hirsh and Billy loaded Floyd up, and Edward watched them drive off with a bad feeling in the pit of his stomach.

Inside the club, he turned the corner and saw George at the bar, counting a small wad of cash.

"Where'd you get that?" Edward asked.

"Mind your own goddamn business," George replied, never looking up.

"This is my goddamn business! Where'd you get the money?"

It couldn't be club money; Edward had all the money from the night's take. And George's eyes carried the dreaded telltale fog. The next question wasn't much of a leap.

"You're supplyin' drugs to our customers aren't ya?"

"Shut the fuck up. What if I am? It's none of your business."

"Does Hirsh know?"

"Why should he? This is no one's business but mine. Why da you think the place is so popular? It's cause of me. They ain't coming here just for the booze and food. I'm the one making this place successful. You and Hirsh don't realize it cause you're too stupid. This club would be nothin' without me."

George went back to counting cash. He quickly finished, tapped the stack into place, and looked back at Edward. "And let me tell you this," he continued in a drug-induced rage, "no one's gonna believe your story anyway. So keep your big mouth shut."

To the side of George's face, Edward said, "If I see you handling drugs, giving out drugs, looking like you're high on drugs ever again, I will take you down myself. We got enough shit to deal with around here. I will not let this club get caught up in a drug scandal."

"Shut the fuck up. You don't even know what you're talking about."

There was no reasoning with someone delusional. George wasn't smart enough to run a bigtime drug business out of the club. That meant he'd be wasting his time trying to talk sense to a low-rent, small-time drug dealer. He turned and left before George could start up his rants again.

While he climbed the stairs to the back office he thought that George must have supplied Floyd with cocaine tonight, cocaine that might well kill him. Hirsh would be livid if he knew, maybe angry enough to finally throw his no-account son-in-law to the curb. George knew Floyd used drugs, everybody at the club knew. But Floyd was never as bad as he was tonight. George took advantage of an easy opportunity to sell Floyd and his party cocaine. Whom else had George sold to?

Edward needed to think about the consequences of telling Hirsh, and he couldn't tell him now anyway, with

Hirsh gone to try to save Floyd's life. With the raid and now Floyd, Edward knew that Hirsh had a lot on his mind. He'd sit on the information for a day or two. He could handle this alone. He just hoped Floyd Guthrie didn't die on the way to the hospital. The last thing the Mayflower Club needed was to be mentioned alongside a coroner's inquest.

* * *

"This son of a bitch." Hirsh looked down at Floyd, who'd started hitching breaths. "Goddammit. Don't die on me." He looked up to the sky. "I did not need this after the night we had." As if someone above was supposed to be looking out for him.

"Where we going boss?"

"Elmwood. It's a small hospital."

Billy drove as quickly as possible, following the directions Hirsh gave, taking care to drive without drawing attention. That meant checking the rearview mirror often. Traffic was light at that hour, and he saw only a few cars here and there. They arrived at the hospital and Hirsh leaped out of the truck and rushed to the emergency entrance.

"I have a friend outside that needs help," Hirsh loudly proclaimed.

Two attendants with a gurney followed Hirsh to his truck.

"He was at my restaurant and passed out. He's been drinking and I think he might be on drugs."

"On drugs?" one of the attendants looked up at Hirsh. "What kind of drugs?"

"How the hell should I know? All's I know is he's been known to take this or that," Hirsh now tried to downplay the declaration.

The two men placed Floyd on the gurney, and one of the men said, "We're going to need you to come inside and provide more information. What's his name?"

"Floyd Guthrie."

The name didn't register with either of them as they proceeded to rush him through the double doors. They surely expected him to follow, but Hirsh didn't intend to stick around. If Floyd lived, he had no idea what the man would provide to the hospital staff.

"Let's go," he said as soon as he rejoined Billy in the truck.

"Don't we need to stick around?" Billy asked.

"Shit no. We need to get the hell outta here is what we need to do. And if anyone asks, you were never here. You got that?"

"Yes, boss."

Hirsh drove Billy to his house, parked the truck two doors down, and asked Billy for the fifteen hundred dollars he needed for LeBeck's. Billy, glad to be relieved of so much money, gave him every last dime. In the commotion of the evening, Hirsh never noticed the car that had been tailing them all night, or the three men inside it. He dropped Billy off and made his way to LeBeck's, unaware that the car continued to follow.

Chapter 21

Washington, DC, 2015

I woke up to the sound of my phone ringing. Or was it my head. Too many martinis. But the ringing didn't stop. I looked over at my phone, realized it was the source and picked it up, thinking it was Clarence.

"Sounds like I woke you." An Australian accent.

"Jaimie … hi. Can you hold just one minute?" I said, trying my best to sound conscious.

"I can call back."

"No. Just give me a second."

I ran to the bathroom, gargled, splashed water on my face, and returned to the phone.

"So sorry. Didn't realize how late it was." I looked at my clock and it was only seven a.m.—which meant four a.m. in California. "You're up early."

"Well, not really. I'm here in DC, on business. I was hoping I could talk you into dinner."

Stalling just for a minute more to clear my head, I asked, "How's your dad doing?"

"Much better, thanks for asking. He's a tough old goat. But the heart attack did take its toll. Fairly sure if I ever want to visit him again, it'll be in Australia. Now, back to the question at hand. I'd love to pick you up this evening for dinner. Do you have plans?"

Despite a pounding headache, I was thinking clearer now. "Glad to hear about your dad. Dinner sounds wonderful. I can meet you somewhere. How'd you know I was here?"

"I called your office. I wasn't sure if you were in Detroit or Washington. I just took a chance and called. I'll pick you up. And in case you're wondering, this is an official date. After all the delays, I'm looking forward to this. Meet you at your hotel at seven. Where are you staying?"

I had to think. "The Hotel Palomar. Near DuPont Circle."

"I know the place. Meet you in the lobby."

Usually I have something witty to say, but this guy still got to me. "Sounds great," was all I could come up with.

"Okay, then. And there'll be no interruptions this time. My cell phone will be turned off. Even you won't be able to reach me to change your mind. So I'll see you tonight."

"Tonight, then." Somehow I liked this direct approach. My heart was pounding. That was ridiculous, I thought, a pounding heart *before* a first date.

Coffee. Now. I hate hotel room coffee, which meant I had to get dressed, throw on makeup, and find the nearest cafe. On my way back to the hotel last night, I'd noticed what I thought might be a coffee shop. It was only a block or two from the hotel. I called Clarence, and we planned to meet at ten. Just enough time to wake up, get rid of the headache, find coffee, and plan the day with him.

I stepped outside. Already hot and humid. The streets were crowded with locals making their way to work. Work. I'd better check in with Beverly.

It wasn't as classy a coffee shop as I remembered. I made it there at least, and ordered a large plain coffee and a greasy bacon-and-egg bagel. Hopefully, the coffee and the bagel would take care of the headache. I gave Beverly a call and as the phone rang, I realized it was only five in the morning in CA. I left a voicemail, finished the bagel, and bought another cup of coffee. One of the bar chairs facing the window opened up. Knowing I had a busy day ahead, I decided to squander a few minutes and gaze out the window. I sat there, sipping steaming-hot coffee, glancing at the crowds of people walking by, headphones on, staring at their phones. The sun reflected on the windowpane. As I soaked it in, I had an unexpected wave of professional uncertainly. I couldn't pinpoint the source. Why was I here again? Oh yes … playing detective. What the hell had I been thinking? I let out a big sigh. So large, the person next to me glanced my way. Ignoring the stare, I continued to stew over my seemingly hasty decision to take this case. As doubt crept into something close to fear of failure, I continued to look out the window. I noticed a man, who looked homeless, playing a guitar. A happy dog, oblivious to the man's plight, dutifully sat next to him, wagging his tail as people stopped, threw some change in a old hat and patted the dog on the head. As if in a trance, I snapped back to reality. I took the last gulp of my coffee, stepped down from the barstool, walked out into the warming sunshine and with uncertain confidence, made my back to the hotel.

As I entered the lobby, Clarence was standing near the check-in counter, coffee in hand.

"Either you're early," I said, "or my phone needs repair." I glanced down at my phone for effect and reassurance. I had a message. I never heard it ring.

"I'm sorry, Miss Mel. I guess I'm anxious to get started. I got here a little early."

"No need to apologize, Clarence. Let me get presentable and I'll be right back down."

"Please don't hurry on my account." He held up the cup. "I'm enjoying my coffee."

"Be down in a few."

In the elevator, I checked the message. Jane in Australia. "All is okay," she'd said. And that she was in Sydney for a few days and to call when I had a chance. What now? I wondered. It was about eleven p.m. in Sydney. I'd call her later today, before my big date.

When next I met Clarence in the lobby, spiffy and fresh, he said, "Where to?"

"Let's hit the library. See what we can find out there." I would've preferred to walk, but doubted Clarence was up to it. The drive was short, and thankfully, there was a parking lot with an open sign near the library. I dropped Clarence off and parked the car.

The Martin Luther King, Jr. Memorial Library is the main public library in DC. There were many smaller branches, but after a few phone calls I'd discovered that all major research was faster and easier at the main branch.

First order of business was a library card. There was a form to fill out and a small fee. Clarence decided to join too. We made our way to the second floor and since my microfiche skills were of the novice type, the clerk helped get me started. He explained that as a member of the library, we could research the *Washington Post* online. Most other newspapers would require microfiche. I gave him a short list of the newspapers I was interested in. One was called the *Afro-American*, one of few Black newspapers in the early 1900s. Clarence decided to take this one on. The newspaper was located in a different room. I gave him dates and names to look up and off he went.

Even though I had access to the *Washington Post* online, I wanted to print pictures of the club if available. As best I could recall, the Mayflower Club opened sometime in the summer of 1933. Not wanting to miss any information, I started in January. It was painstaking work, yet fascinating. I found myself getting lost in stories that had nothing to do with the Mayflower Club. There were advertisements for ladies' clothes, and elixirs to help with hair, headaches, and various ailments. The NY Rangers beat the Toronto Maple Leafs for the Stanley Cup. The Chicago Bears played their first NFL game. Walt Disney released *The Three Little Pigs*. The FDR presidency and all the controversy behind the New Deal. Hangings, Jim Crow laws, the KKK. I could've spent days there.

I finally saw the first article about the club.

The Mayflower Club Raided

Mr. Hirsh Rosenburg along with Mr. Edward Higgins were part of a raid of the swanky Mayflower Club on Connecticut Avenue. The Feds obtained 30 quarts of liquor, champagne, and wine. They found printed menus with 50-cent drinks and $10 champagne …

And then this one.

Owner of the Mayflower Club Robbed

Mr. Hirsh Rosenburg, the owner of the swanky Mayflower Club, was robbed yesterday at gunpoint as he stepped off the elevator in his Woodley Park Towers complex. It's believed the men got away with at least $1,500 in cash, checks, and gold. Neighbors heard a scuffle and called police. Mr. Rosenburg was found bound and gagged. No arrests have been made.

I made copies of every article I could find in hopes to further piece together the history of the club. I wasn't sure how helpful this information would be, but it corroborated Clarence's claims. I was a bit surprised when I noticed we'd been at the research for almost five hours. It was time to take a break and check on Clarence. I walked down the hall and found him hunched over the microfiche reader. I tapped him on the shoulder and he jumped.

"Engrossing isn't it," I said.

"I'm sorry, Miss Mel. I was so involved in these articles," he replied with a bashful smile. "I think I forgot where I was."

"Do you know we've been here for almost five hours? Hard to believe. Have you had any luck with information about your Uncle Edward?"

"I found a little bit. There was an article about a raid on the club in November of 1933."

"I think I found a similar article, and others too. I made copies to take back to the hotel and try to piece together the information." I sighed. "The results of the arrest and raids, they're hardly mentioned. I did make it through 1933, but there are other newspapers I'd like to look at too. And I didn't even get to 1934. Let's go get some lunch at the hotel and compare notes."

"I can be ready to go in five minutes," Clarence said. "Soon as I figure how to mark my place on this thing."

"Okay. Meet you downstairs."

As I made my way to the elevator, my mind slipped to thoughts of my date with Jaimie. It'd been a while since we last saw each other. And we'd only met briefly. What if I wasn't what he remembered? What if I got that disappointed look? What if we had a drink at the hotel and he pulled the "I just remembered I have to go somewhere" line? What was I going to wear? I forgot what I'd packed. I—

"Ready to go," Clarence snapped me back into reality.

"Oh, ah … yes."

Clarence wasn't the type to notice or ask what was on my mind, and I was thankful for that right now. We drove back to the hotel, and then walked to a tiny restaurant nearby for a late lunch.

"Okay," I started. "Here's what I found out. Edward Higgins worked for a man named Hirsh Rosenburg. Hirsh Rosenburg owned the club. As far as I can tell, the club opened in early 1933. There was an article about a raid on the club late that year, and another article about Mr. Rosenburg being robbed. The article mentions the alcohol, but not the gambling. Either the government didn't find the gambling equipment or it didn't exist."

"It was there all right. Uncle Edward said most of the money came from gambling. He said they didn't keep accurate records on the gambling money but it was substantial. I wish I knew what *substantial* meant to him. He said they did keep track of how much they made selling liquor."

"What were those three letters we found in the ledger book? 'A', 'G' and something else. The 'A' could stand for alcohol and the 'G' for gaming I guess."

"The other letter was an 'O.' Maybe that stood for 'other'?"

"That would be fairly simple. Still doesn't help much," I said. "We'll take a look at the figures when we get back. I'm still not sure how your uncle was able to accumulate so much money over such a short period of time."

Clarence looked to the ground and then back up at me with a worried expression.

"Is there something else I should know, Clarence?"

"Miss Mel. There's a bit more to the story. I wasn't sure I could trust you completely, but maybe I should tell you the rest now."

He paused as if deciding how much to spill. Then he said, "I'm quite sure my uncle was also involved somehow in drugs."

"Drugs. What do you mean, drugs? Using, selling?"

"I don't think he took them. No I don't. But I do believe that one of managers of the club was involved in selling drugs at the club, and Uncle Edward was somehow involved."

"So you think that some of this money is drug money?"

"Some of it, maybe. My uncle talked about getting money for powder. I was a kid and had no idea what 'powder' was. Lookin' back, I'm fairly sure they were talking about cocaine. I did some research while I was at the library, and in wasn't uncommon for speakeasies to have a drug business on the side."

"Well, that could explain additional money, for sure. The arrests don't mention drugs, though. At least in the articles I've read thus far. That would be bit more … nefarious."

"I don't know his involvement. Maybe none at all. I just wanted to let you know."

"I would've appreciated knowing this from the start. Just so you know, it wouldn't have changed my mind, but still I like to know all the facts or so-called facts. Is there anything else I should be aware of?"

He took a deep breath and seemed not to want to release it, but did. "Yes, one more thing I should tell you. I believe Edward killed a man."

"Killed a man, you say. Your uncle was a piece of work. Can you elaborate?"

"He said he killed a cracker in self-defense."

"Okay, just so I'm clear, that would be a white man?"

"Yes it would, Miss Mel. I'm just quotin' him. He said it several times. He said the man was trying to rob him. He said he buried the man himself, in a little cemetery."

"Well, that would be consistent with the picture you showed me. Do you know if this is the guy who stole all his money?"

"I believe it was, but my uncle never made a whole lotta sense."

"And if the guy did steal the money and he's dead, then where is it? The money I mean."

"I know it looks like a dead end. I truly know it looks grim. But I believe the money is hidden somewhere, and we're just missin' a few clues. Dorothy knows more than she's saying. And I know a place we can start looking."

"Where's that?"

"Remember the drawing I showed you while we were in Detroit? It looked like a cemetery?"

I nodded

"I think I know where it is. It's called Whispering Pines."

Chapter 22

Washington, DC, 1933

As Hirsh drove to LeBeck's, he thought he noticed a car following him. He took a few wrong turns. The car followed. No sense in leading anyone to his liquor distributor. He decided to head toward his apartment and see if they followed.

He pulled up to his building; the car passed by. Concerned that they might come back, Hirsh decided to park and wait. Remembering the money, he hid it in his coat pocket. He waited a few minutes, saw no one, and decided he was being paranoid. Likely from fatigue. "The best cure for that is sleep," he muttered as he got out of the truck. He planned to catch a few hours sleep and then head to LeBeck's.

As he was about to unlock the door to his apartment, he felt something hard shoved into his back and a blow to his head that left his ears ringing.

"Don't move or you're dead," a man's voice ordered. "Put your hands up where we can see 'em."

We? Hirsh reluctantly raised his hands. A man reached around from behind him and began ruffling through Hirsh's pockets. When his hand felt the lump in Hirsh's coat, he reached in and pulled out the moneybag, and opened it. Hirsh thought about shifting his body, trying to see if he recognized either assailant, but the gun jammed in his back and one of the men growling, "It would be wise for your health if you did not turn around," made him think again.

Hirsh remained silent but his mind roiled, considering the loss. There must be at least fifteen hundred dollars in the bag. It wasn't a severe hit to the club, he rationalized, but he was nonetheless irate at his recklessness at not following a procedure he demanded of others. As he stood there, hands still in the air, he heard someone run down the stairs. Still feeling the poke in his back, he remained still.

"Open the door," the man said.

Hirsh eased one hand down and turned the knob, and heard the man say, "Get inside."

One of the men directed him to a chair. As he sat, he stole a glance at the two men. No help. Both wore masks. Millie was with her ailing mom. Thank goodness she wasn't at the apartment. God knew what might've happened if she was here right now.

Within a minute, he was gagged and tied to the chair. "That should take care of your motherfuckin' ass," one of the men said. Both men opened closets, cupboards, and drawers, tossing everything on the floor. All Hirsh could do was watch. Satisfied there was nothing else to find, they headed for the door. Hirsh watched them open the door and take one last look to make sure he was still tied up, and then he watched as they closed the door.

Though he blamed his aching head, he quickly learned that his assailants knew what they were doing; the ties binding him to the chair were too tight for him to even try to free himself. Now he regretted his earlier thought about Millie not being home. His only option was to wait for someone to arrive, wincing occasionally from the head wound and hoping the blood he felt running down his neck didn't mean he was bleeding to death.

It wasn't long before he heard sirens. When the pounding came on the door, he did his best to make a sound, any sound. The effort caused him to briefly lose consciousness. He barely heard the cops burst open the door to find him bound and gagged. Struggling for what to say, his head screaming with pain, he was coherent enough to make up a lie.

One of the cops said, "Your neighbors called after they heard a commotion. You're one lucky man. What happened mister?"

"I-I guess I was followed home, officers. I own a restaurant nearby and … this is gonna sound stupid, but I removed all my money from the safe. To take to the bank in the morning," he lied. "About fifteen hundred."

The officer's eyes widened. "Dollars?"

Hirsh nodded, winced, and continued the lie. "Yeah. My whole month's take. I don't know what I'm gonna do."

The other cop came closer, withdrew his handkerchief, and pressed it to the back of Hirsh's head. "Well that's a shame. Can you identify any of the ones who did this to you?"

"Unfortunately not." He needed to get rid of the cops and get to LeBeck's to pay his debt. "I was pretty much knocked out the whole time. I'm so upset by this," Hirsh said, trying to look as distraught as possible.

The cops stayed for a while, took fingerprints, and surveyed the apartment for clues, asking question after question. All useless, Hirsh knew, but he stayed quiet and tried to look distressed. Which wasn't that difficult to pull off.

"Listen mister," one of the cops said in a consoling manner, "you haven't given us much to go on, but maybe the fingerprints will bring up something. We need you to come downtown and make an official statement."

That couldn't happen; Hirsh had more urgent matters to take care of. "I'll be down later this morning. Let me get a few hours' rest."

"That gash looks pretty bad," the other cops said. "You should have it looked at."

"I'll call my wife. She's with her sick mother. She can take care of it." Not a complete lie.

After the cops left, Hirsh went into the bathroom to look at the gash. It did look pretty bad. He ran the sink cold and threw a handful of water on it, winced, and grabbed a towel to help with the bleeding, wondering if there was some kind of bandage anywhere in the apartment. His head was hurting but he knew he had to get over to LeBeck's. The financial loss wouldn't cripple the restaurant, but he still owed LeBeck the money. One rule he lived by was to never, ever piss off his liquor distributor. Exhausted and looking as battered as he felt, one hand holding the towel, one on the wheel, Hirsh began the drive to LeBeck's, without the money.

This time he kept an eye on his rearview mirror. The streets were empty. He was fairly confident he wasn't followed this time. Head pounding, he drove the truck around to the back of LeBeck's, checked around him one last time, got out and made his way to the back entrance. He found LeBeck in the warehouse's office.

"What the hell happened to you?" LeBeck asked as soon as he saw Hirsh.

"Got robbed."

"Well that's a mighty shame. Where's my money?"

"I was on my way here when it happened. I know this looks bad, but I ain't never missed a payment. Didn't want to blow you off. I'll have the money tonight."

LeBeck's expression darkened. "Never known you to be robbed before."

Dizziness threatened to overtake Hirsh. "Look, my head … mind if we sit down?"

With one finger, LeBeck pointed to the ratty, stained visitor's chair and took the one behind the desk. The dizziness ebbed as soon as Hirsh sat down. The pain in his head, not so much.

"Floyd Guthrie got tanked at the club. We thought he might die and I didn't need the cops snoopin' around. Not after the raid we had a few nights ago. We drove him to the hospital and I must've been tailed."

"Floyd Guthrie? You should've let the shithead die and thrown him in the streets."

"Like I said, I wasn't sure if he was gonna die."

"Sounds like a streak of bad luck. May it not continue."

"I've had worse. I got the money. I'll bring it by tonight after the restaurant closes."

"I'll be expecting you."

"I need more whisky. We've been packed every night."

"If you want the booze, bring the money before you open tonight and I'll have it ready. Say the word 'early' to the guard and I'll let you in. Just this once."

"Look, Pete …"

"Bring the money tonight. No earlier than nine. I'm takin' a big risk, ya know."

Hirsh could tell that LeBeck wasn't budging. No sense in wasting time. "I'll have your money tonight."

"That would be wise."

The sun was starting to come up. Hirsh got back in his car, checked again for a tail, didn't find one, and drove to the club. As he drove, it struck him. Millie. If she'd come back to the apartment already … seen the blood, the chair, the fingerprint dust … she had to be wondering where he was. He'd call her from the club. But he wasn't sure he'd be able to tell her how a night, that started out on such a high note, had ended in disaster.

His head throbbing, he arrived at the club, went inside, sat at the same table where they found Floyd, and passed out.

Chapter 23

 *Washington, DC, 2015*

As I stepped into my hotel room, my mind began to shift from the day's events at the library to my date with Jaimie. So far there was no phone call cancelling the date, and no emergencies from home. Good signs. I began to think this date might actually happen. My watch told me I had a few hours to get ready. And a bath was in order. While waiting for the tub to fill, I checked over my wardrobe, which for a change, looked more appropriate for a dig than a date. Every single item far too casual for DC, nightlife. Except … when I dug down, I remembered that I did bring a few dresses.

The black-and-red dress matched the new black heels. They weren't date-like, meaning seductive and high, but that was what I had to work with. I looked at the underwear I'd packed. Not good. What if things progressed? The bra and panties didn't match, but too late to worry about it now.

Having solved all the wardrobe problems, I decided a drink was in order to calm my nerves. I called down to room service and ordered a bottle of Prosecco. Nothing like the soothing effect of a glass of Italian champagne.

After the champagne arrived, I slipped into the tub and took stock of my trip. Murder, money, and drugs. Discoveries made on many archeological digs, but this time the discoveries affected those still living. They affected a person I was coming to care about as I would an uncle.

As it turned out, the stakes were higher than I originally thought. Maybe more than I could handle. Maybe time to get another opinion? My mom was out of the question and if I told my kids, they'd worry and tell me to dump the case. Which meant leaving Clarence to whatever wolves were out there, which I wouldn't do. Depending on how the night went, I thought I might run it by Jaimie.

I dressed, took stock of my looks, approved without reservation, and made my way downstairs a few minutes early. Not earlier than Jaimie, though—he sat at the bar, two glasses of champagne on the table. And I also saw Clarence, seated not far away. Clarence saw me first. I didn't want to ignore him so I stopped to say hello. Jaimie noticed me, yet remained at the bar. I finished my brief hello and as I started walking toward Jaimie, he stood.

He greeted me with a kiss on the cheek. "It's been too long since our first visit in Australia. You look beautiful."

Jaimie was wearing a dark suit, a pink paisley tie and a grin that would melt butter. My heart was pounding, so much so, I hoped Jaimie didn't notice. I really had nothing witty to say. I stayed with the tried-and-true. "I'm glad we finally have the chance to see each other." Unoriginal but accurate.

With Clarence nearby, it seemed rude not to introduce him, so I said, "I'd like you to meet someone." I walked Jaimie over to Clarence's table.

"Clarence, I'd like to introduce you to Jaimie. We met in Australia while I was there visiting one of my sites. Clarence and I are working on a project here in Washington," I said looking at Jaimie.

"A pleasure to meet you, Jaimie," Clarence said as he shook Jaimie's hand.

"I'd like to hear more about this project." Jaimie had looked my way.

"Maybe later," I said, and shifted my gaze to Clarence, who said, "Miss Mel, have a nice evening," and left the bar.

We sat down for a few minutes. I nervously drank the glass of bubbly. After we'd finished our drinks, and exchanged a few pleasantries, Jaimie took my hand and we headed to the entrance. "I've made reservations nearby. Thought we'd take a stroll."

"Perfect."

We discussed his sister and father. I gave him an update on my daughter's impromptu wedding and a few details regarding my archeology project in Australia. We arrived at the restaurant and as we were being escorted to our table, Jaimie gently kissed my neck. A bit forward, I thought, but tingled just the same, and decided this could be a fun night.

We ordered appetizers, for which I had no appetite, and cocktails, which I needed desperately, and while we waited for the waiter to return with our drinks, Jaimie asked me about Clarence.

"It's a bit complicated," I said. "And I can't say too much—he's a client, after all. But he showed up at my office in LA. He persuaded me to take on a case that's ... slightly out of my professional experience. Okay, more than slightly. It seems he had an uncle who worked in a speakeasy in the 1930s. But more than working at the club, he was the right-hand man to a man named Hirsh Rosenburg. Hirsh managed the club and Edward, that's Clarence's uncle, might have been involved in some crimes." I paused for a moment, decided how much more to reveal, then continued. "Through details that are too lengthy for tonight, Clarence thinks there's a substantial amount of club money hidden and he asked me to help locate it."

Jaimie's attention never wavered. "That's quite the story. Any success in solving the mystery?"

"Have we found any money? Not yet. And I'm not convinced I'm heading in the right direction. Mr. Rosenburg had a granddaughter who's still alive. We went to visit her, she lives in an extravagant old folks' home, and after our discussion, I'm convinced she's holding back information. She's old, but still has plenty of smarts. I think we can get more information out of her. And we have some material evidence that corroborates the story. I spent time at the library today, in fact. Discovered some tidbits about the club. But it feels like we're stalled."

Jaimie considered this. "I'm here for a few days. Any way I can help?"

"Well ... you've already helped by listening. Although the whole scenario must sound like a Hollywood script."

He chuckled. "More like a 'facts are stranger than fiction' scenario. But really, I want to help if I can."

"Let me think about that. Maybe. The amount of corruption going on seems insurmountable. But I'm not one to give up. I finally hired a decent assistant in LA. She handling my archeology business. Actually, this has been a good challenge for me. It's widened my thinking about my career. Quite frankly, I needed the change. If I'm successful here, I might add detective work to my business. But that's down the road a bit. First, I have to help Clarence if I can."

"My advice? Isn't an archeologist a detective? Just looking for something a bit different, is all. Any danger here?"

"Oh, I doubt it. This happened almost seventy-five years ago." I decided not to tell Jaimie about the incident with the flooring guy. Not sure why. It just didn't seem important.

"Where is this club?" Jaimie asked.

"It's actually not far from here. It's a restaurant now, but back in the 1930s it was a gin joint called Mayflower Club."

"Maybe we should stop in for a drink after dinner," Jaimie suggested.

"I like that idea," I said, knowing that would also extend the date past dinner. "Can you tell me more about the Warner Brothers project? This'll probably sound ridiculous, but I had high hopes of running into someone famous when I dropped off your proposal. You must see movie stars all the time."

"Honestly I do, and you are being ridiculous. Not a big deal." I frowned at him and he laughed. "Okay, that might have been harsh. I forget that I work in this business, and that's all it is with me. Business. Next time I'm on a movie shoot, I'll invite you along. You will be completely bored with the process."

"Somehow that type of boredom sounds appealing. I also meant to tell you that your apartment is spectacular. And very secure."

The server arrived with our food, and I expected Jaimie to forget what I'd said about his place by the time we were eating. He didn't.

"I don't live there for the security, I assure you. Some of the residents might need it, but please don't think it's me. My dad originally bought several apartments in the building. For a company write-off. Besides, he needed a place to stay when in LA and since it was secure, and he traveled a lot, he felt comfortable there. Too grand for me really." He shrugged. "But I've taken over the place, all my stuff is there, and I'm too lazy to move. It really boils down to that."

"I have to admit, I felt like a criminal at first. But got over it after I stepped inside. Who's the decorator?"

He smiled. "That would be Bette. I had nothing to do with it. But I do love the view."

"How is your dad?"

"He is better, but there is limited travel in his future. My two sisters will take over the care responsibilities. And me when I can get back there. Dad's fine on his own, but we've hired a twenty-four-hour nurse and there is always staff around. And if you think that apartment was fancy, you should see his place. Palatial. I could never live in something that big now. We grew up there, though, and he refuses to move. I prefer living in the States, but," he looked down, then back up, "I'll have to spend more time in Australia now.

This Warner Brothers project looks like a go for us though, so I'll be in LA and Sydney for three or four months."

A man like this in my life for three, maybe four months? I could enjoy that. "What's the project? Can you talk about it?"

"I can now. It's been greenlighted, which means the project can move forward. It's a comedy about a couple from LA who buys a thriving restaurant chain in Australia. They know nothing about Australia or the restaurant business. The script has been reworked for several years, which is common and frustrating all at the same time. Warner Brothers is using an outside production company to help with the shooting in Australia, and they chose us. We've worked together before, and I thought we were a shoo-in until another production company snuck in at the last minute. Dealing with Warner and Dad got a bit tricky. Really glad it's resolved for now."

"So you'll be working in LA?" I said, hoping.

"Mostly. I'm here in DC, scouting some locations. Apparently one of the characters has a brother that's ..." he raised his eyebrows in jest, "a US Senator!"

I laughed. "Sounds like an interesting plot."

"I haven't had much chance to read the complete script, but if they get the actors they're mentioning, the picture has a shot. My staff handles the minor details, but I've learned to get the major details out of the way first."

Jaimie asked about my kids, and I gladly told them all the details about their lives and working for me, which naturally brought us back to my business. I told him about Beverly and my hope to make her more of a partner than assistant.

Nodding, he said, "Yes, that's right thinking. A partner has a stake in a business, but only the most loyal employees feel that connected."

We finished dinner and Jaimie was still interested, so we headed to the Dirty Martini. I decided to tell him as little as I could about the place. Although it was certainly nothing like the Mayflower Club, for some reason, I wanted to get his impression of the place without my preconceived ideas.

As we walked through the front door, Jack greeted us. "Back so soon? That must have been some martini."

I smiled at him. "I think it was more the excellent service."

"You are a lucky man to be in the company of such a beautiful woman," Jack said, looking at Jaimie.

"Oh, I think he just wanted a good martini," I said through an embarrassed chuckle.

"No, he's right," Jaimie said. "Okay, maybe on both counts." Jaimie smiled my way and took my hand as we followed Jack to a table near the bar area.

The restaurant was noticeably busier than my last visit. Jack helped me with my chair and after he left to have our martinis delivered, I gave Jaimie the history of the club.

"As best I can research, the Mayflower Club opened in the summer of 1933. Prohibition was still around. No liquor allowed in public places. Not only did they drink here, but they also gambled as well. Games and booze were on the third floor. The restaurant is located where we're sitting now. See the mirror behind me?"

He nodded and fixed his gaze on the mirror. "How could I miss it? It's fantastic!"

"It might also hold a clue to the mystery. Clarence found paperwork that references the mirror and a box stashed behind it."

Eyebrows raised again, but not in jest. "Have you looked?"

"Not yet. I'm not even sure how to get behind the mirror, especially one that big. And I don't see any opening or door through it—to get behind it, it would have to be damaged. I'm not ready to ask anyone here either. Not just yet. No sense arousing suspicion. Which sounds paranoid, I know. But something tells me not to. Clarence and I are going to snoop around early one morning. I really doubt anything is still there, clues or no clues. It can't be that simple."

Jaimie nodded, thoughtful. "That would be convenient."

"When I was here last time, I was given a tour. Said I knew this was the Mayflower Club at one time, and was a history buff. I'm sure I know more historical information than they do. They showed me the back rooms on the third floor, and the secret elevator used to shuffle clients between the first and third floors. I just acted like an interested tourist."

Jaimie looked at our empty glasses and extended a hand, smiling. "Let's take a look around."

I took Jaimie upstairs, and showed him the hallways where the offices were located. He agreed that the view from the upstairs loft to the restaurant downstairs, the mirror prominently positioned, was quite a sight.

As we made our way back down to our table, Jaimie took my hand and said, "I know a great place for coffee. Interested?"

I wasn't entirely sure if he meant now or later. To play it safe, I said I was.

Our waiter stopped by and Jaimie asked for the check. We finished our drinks and began walking back to my hotel.

"My car is parked at your hotel," he said. "Let's take a drive and find that coffee place."

I wanted to extend the evening, but not at a coffee shop. Time to push the envelope. "I have a better idea. My room is a suite and there's a perfect little coffeemaker conveniently inside."

Jaimie stopped walking, turned toward me, met my eyes, and gently kissed my lips, but didn't immediately draw his away. As if in a dream state, I realized I wanted that kiss to continue, but abruptly he pulled back and took my hand, and we finished the walk to the hotel.

There was a nervous silence as we walked into the room, neither of us knowing exactly what would happen next, just the direction we were heading. Jaimie took both of my hands in his and said, "I think we both may want the coffee to wait?" A question that needed no answer. And he kissed me gently again, drawing out a tingle that covered every inch of my body. He reached for my zipper and began unzipping my dress. He stopped just for a second or two and when he realized I was happily on board, the zipper came all the way down. As we began kissing again, I literally had no idea where I was. My head was spinning, the anticipation for this moment intoxicating.

I began to unbutton his shirt but decided to keep with his slow pace, instead of what I really wanted, which was to rip the shirt off, buttons be damned. I removed his shirt and reached for his belt. He met my eyes, as if to again make sure

I wanted this. I'd never had a man who seemed concerned about what I wanted before. Strange, but all I could think was, why was he still single? Attractive, wealthy, and now add caring? I must be in for major heartbreak. But this moment was too enthralling to let my thoughts get in the way.

* * *

I had no idea how much time passed but after we finally fell apart, I was euphorically exhausted. Jaimie looked like he needed a cigarette.

My first words: "Do you smoke?"

After a few seconds of laughter, Jaimie said, "Now what made you say that?"

"You know, after every exceptional sex scene in the movies, the guy smokes."

"For the record, I don't smoke, but if I did, I'd be lighting up right about now."

"I might want to do that again."

"That was the goal." He reached over and gave me a kiss.

"I could make that coffee we talked about?"

"Or you could stay right here. That's my vote."

"I have to ask. How is it that you aren't engaged or attached? Or are you any of those ... things?"

With a sigh, he leaned back on his elbows. "I've been married and it didn't go too well. I caught my wife cheating on me with an old boyfriend. I knew better. Yet I still married her. I have to admit now, it took a while to recover. It was my family that had a mini intervention. Sent me to the States to run our operation here ... well, in LA. Best thing they could've done. I date, but I like to blame my schedule from committing to anything long term."

"Ah ha. Guess your schedule is about to become really busy," I said … mostly joking. Mostly.

"Aren't you the funny one? We both seem to have a plate full."

"That's actually, full plate," I said. "And of course you're right."

"Now you know about me. And you?"

"In a nutshell, recently happily unattached, and I must add, better for it."

There was silence. A little longer than I was comfortable with.

"Jaimie, here's what I think. We're no doubt busy people. I get that. I'm certainly attracted to you. For the record, I don't think I'm high maintenance. I'd like to stay in touch and start there."

More silence. Until he said, "For the record, you're adorable. And it's been a long time since I've felt this way. Quite relaxed actually. Sex withstanding," he looked directly at me and took my hand, "I want you to feel that you can call me. Let's take this time to get to know each other. It won't happen if we worry about how often we communicate."

"I can work with that. How about texting? Are we good with texting? I mean, I am a known over-texter."

He laughed that laugh I already didn't think I could do without. "Okay, that's pushing it. But I'll work with it."

"Look, we're two bright people. I think we'll figure this out, or we won't. I had a fantastic time. And just so you know, I liked helping you with the proposal for Warner

Brothers. Maybe you can give me a more in-depth tour of your apartment. There were quite a few cameras in the building. I was afraid to breathe."

"I owe you that, at the least. And just so you know, there are no cameras in my apartment."

I looked at the clock. Four-thirty a.m. I had to meet Clarence at seven.

"Would you like to stay?"

He swiveled his head to meet my eyes. "I would love to stay, but I need you to miss me and that won't happen while I'm here."

Chapter 24

 *Washington, DC, 1933*

Hirsh woke up to the sound of footsteps.

"You okay boss?"

Hirsh looked up from the booth, never more grateful to see Edward's face. "Yeah." He laid his head back down and tried to return to sleep, remembered he couldn't. "What time is it?"

"Almost nine thirty."

Hirsh sat up and Edward saw the head gash. "What happened to you boss?"

"Got robbed last night."

"Here?"

"No. In my building."

Edward walked over to Hirsh. "Looks like they roughed you up pretty good. Maybe you should see a doc?"

"I'll be all right. But we lost LeBeck's money. I was stupid. We dropped Floyd off at the hospital. They must'a been following me since I left the restaurant. Too busy with Floyd to notice. Still don't know how they figured I had money. Maybe just a lucky guess."

"Maybe."

"Someone called the cops. I made it sound like they took a month of restaurant receipts. We lost fifteen hundred bucks. I didn't want them sniffin' 'round here. We've had too much heat lately."

"Get any kind of look at 'em?"

"Not enough."

Millie walked through the front door, saw Hirsh slumped over in the booth, and let out a dramatic gasp before hurrying to him. "Hirsh my baby, what happened?"

"I told you on the phone. Nothing happened. Just a small robbery."

"A small robbery? Well who'da heard of such a thing. Small robbery. Every robbery is big. Look at your head. You need to see a doctor."

"I told him that too," Edward chimed in. "Says he won't go."

She looked at Hirsh and then back at Edward. "I'll make him go."

"Nobody is making me do nothin'. I'm fine," Hirsh moaned.

Millie asked Edward, "Is there a first aid kit in here?"

"Underneath the bar on the right," Edward pointed.

While Millie went for the first aid kit, Billy and George walked through the door.

"What happened boss?" Billy asked.

Edward looked at Billy. "I'll tell you later."

George, ignoring the situation at hand, merely walked past Hirsh and headed up the stairs.

First aid kit in hand, Millie walked back toward Hirsh. She opened the kit and, finding a bottle of peroxide, she knew enough to dab a piece of cotton with the sanitizer and gently clean the wound. She dug around the kit looking for the largest Band-Aid she could find and with a gentle hand, she covered the cut with the bandage.

"There," she proudly proclaimed. "That should help keep the germs out. Would you like an aspirin? There's a whole tin of 'em in here."

Hirsh gave her a kiss. "No thanks, doll, I got work to do. If your mom is feelin' better, why don't you come back later tonight? I'll buy you a bottle of champagne. I've got some big boys comin' in tonight and I could use you here."

"Mom says she's still sick. But I don't think it's that bad. You need to take a nap or somethin'. You look kinda worn out." She looked around the room. "Let these guys do all the work for once."

Everyone ignored her slight. No sense in stirring up trouble.

"Doll, I'll see you tonight," Hirsh said, pecked her on the cheek, and with all the energy he could muster, he stood, trying to steady himself, and walked toward Edward.

"Look, I need to pay LeBeck and we need to pick up some whiskey. We're really low. I'll need you and Billy to go with me. Plan on leavin' just after dark. Pete said he could meet us at nine."

"Don't we have enough for tonight, boss? Pickin' up at night is—"

"Do you think I'd fuckin' risk it if we did?" Hirsh said, irritated. He placed his hand over the bandage and winced. After a moment or two he said "we'll take the truck. Make sure you bring a gun. You and I will have guns. Billy's too green."

"Yes boss." Edward knew there was no chance of changing his mind.

"And help me keep a lookout tonight. I don't know who was followin' me, but I gotta keep better track on what's goin' on. Tell George he's watchin' the club while we're gone."

Edward simply nodded. The thought of leaving George alone in the club was concerning. Trouble could come from that.

Edward found George behind the bar. "Billy, boss, and me are goin' on an errand tonight. Boss said to tell you that you got the club." He noticed George's hands shaking, his bloodshot eyes. "You okay?"

"Mind your own goddamned business. Not much sleep is all."

"Well you better be awake tonight."

"Don't worry about me. And don't be snitchin' to Hirsh. I know you hate me and you think you run this place. But you ain't shit. Remember who's married to the boss's daughter. If you had any smarts, and you don't, you'd be lookin' for a new place to work. You ain't long for here. Boss has me in charge now."

It cost him, but Edward gave George a noncommittal stare and walked away. He believed there was no truth in George's drug fueled rant. And he still had no concrete proof that George was using drugs. At least not yet. He reminded himself to keep closer tabs on George. The thought of telling Hirsh that his alcoholic daughter's husband was a junkie was not an appealing one, but that was for another day.

He found Billy on the third floor busy polishing the roulette wheel to its usual high shine. "Billy, we're goin' on an errand tonight. Need you to come along. Probably leave close to nine."

"Where we goin'?"

"I'll tell you on the way."

Chapter 25

Washington, DC, 2015

I don't remember sleeping but must have drifted off. The alarm blared at six. I raced through a shower and somehow managed to pull it all together. Clarence was at the bar with two cups of coffee. He nudged one my way.

"I may be old but somehow I knew you'd need this," Clarence said. Apparently, I felt more chipper than I looked.

"It was a long night, but I'm eager to get started. I feel like we just might make some progress in the next few days."

"I hope so."

"I thought we'd head over to the restaurant first, while the outside crowd is light and before any employees show up. Then we can drive to Whispering Pines for a look-see. Do you have the cemetery map?"

Clarence patted his pocket. "Right here."

"When I briefly toured the restaurant, I noticed an alleyway. Let's start there."

The sun was just beginning to peek over the buildings, and it felt good to be moving. Clarence and I arrived at the club. There were a few people milling about in the area, but the club itself looked closed. We walked by the entrance and didn't see anyone around. I'd never noticed any cameras outside but wanted to be sure. I peeked in the window and could see the dining area. All lights were off.

Clarence and I walked around to the back and found the alcove I'd seen on my last visit. Again, I looked for cameras, and didn't see any. There was just enough light to see to the back of the alcove.

We walked down to the end of the alcove. I didn't notice anything out of the ordinary. We walked back and forth several times, and still saw nothing. I recalled that the mirror was located on the same wall as the alcove. As I bent down to take a closer look, I noticed something off about the outside bricks. One in particular.

"Clarence, come here."

I tried to wiggle the brick, but it wouldn't budge. There was definite cracking in the mortar but the space was too small to move the brick.

"We need a knife or something," I said.

Clarence produced a Swiss Army knife.

"That was easy." I jammed the knife in the mortar; the brick moved slightly. Not enough to loosen it from the wall, though. I had to go back and forth with the knife for what seemed an eternity before we were finally able grab the brick and pull it out. It was too dark to see inside the space we created. I looked at the bricks around it. The grout between them was old and crumbling. We were able to remove six more bricks.

And then, we hit pay dirt. Inside the space, just in back of where the bricks would have been, sitting by itself, was a medium-sized gray tin box. "I'm so surprised to find anything," I said to Clarence, "I'm not quite sure what to do."

Clarence took over and reached for the box. We looked around to make sure no one was watching us. We didn't see anyone. Clarence held the box and turned it to where its front faced us. "There's a key lock," he said in a low voice. We looked at each other.

"Did you bring the key?" I asked.

"It's in the hotel room."

I took the box from him. Curious, I shook it. There was something inside. Sounded like paper.

"We have to take this with us," I said, knowing he felt the same way.

Before I replaced the bricks, I looked inside to make sure I hadn't missed anything. The bricks on the other side appeared to be loose too. Hard to notice unless you really looked. "Clarence, come here, see what I see? That must lead to the inside of the club."

He withdrew his face from the opening. "I think you're right, Miss Mel."

We put the bricks back. Mortar had fallen and we had nothing to clean the area.

I took a tissue out of my purse and tried pushing as much as I could against the wall, where it would be less likely to be seen and make someone curious. As I came to the conclusion I'd done my best, Clarence walked to the end of the alley. He looked both ways.

"Are you ready, Miss Mel?"

Holding the box, I joined him, thinking that this felt clandestine. I'd now stolen something. I'd just added to my breaking and entering rap sheet. But this was no time to contemplate my crimes. I looked down at the box and realized we couldn't just carry it back to the hotel. Logically no one would question the box. But logic wasn't playing a strong role here. We'd have to hide it.

I pointed to his coat. "Take off your coat. We'll hide it underneath."

* * *

There were people walking by us as we emerged from the alcove. No one seemed interested, but I didn't want to risk anything now. We picked up our pace to a brisk walk until we reached the hotel.

As we entered the lobby, I suggested we go to Clarence's room. What I didn't say was that mine was in a bit of disarray from the previous night's activities. But perhaps he guessed that.

After he secured the door to his room, I set the box on the table. Clarence retrieved the key and we both stared at each other. Neither of us thought the key would fit as he placed the key into the lock, jiggled it just enough that the rust from the lock jogged loose, and the key turned the lock. As if looking for approval to continue, Clarence looked my way. I gave him the universal nod and he opened the box.

Inside, we found a single piece of paper. Clarence and I again looked at each other, not sure which of us wanted to take the paper out. What if it meant nothing? What if it was blank? Indecipherable? What if this was another dead end?

I reached in for the paper, which had been folded into quarters who knew how long ago? I unfolded it and held it where Clarence could see it too, and we stared at it.

Clarence looked at me. I looked at him, and we both returned our gazes to the contents on the paper.

"What do you suppose that means?" Clarence said, his voice hushed.

Chapter 26

Washington, DC, 1933

Edward looked at his pocket watch. "Time to go," he yelled in Billy's direction.

Billy looked up to the second floor and saw Hirsh coming down the stairs—and the bulge of the gun he'd placed in his coat pocket.

"Don't I need a gun too?" Billy said.

"No, son, you'll be fine. I'm leaving you in the truck while we get the booze. I don't need you shootin' no one."

The three of them loaded into the truck. "Keep a look out, Edward," Hirsh said.

The streets were quiet for a Saturday evening. It had been raining all day and a light mist continued to fall. As they made their way to LeBeck's, they detoured on side roads hoping to lessen the risk of being followed.

"Stop here," Hirsh said to Billy. Billy shifted his eyes to Hirsh, confused. They were still about a block from LeBeck. "I wanna make sure we weren't followed."

They waited for a few minutes, Hirsh keeping a vigil on the rearview mirror. Seeing nothing, he nodded and pointed through the windshield, and Billy pulled back onto the street. Moments later they were near the back entrance to the building.

"Pull around the corner and wait," he said to Billy. "Don't stick around if you see trouble. I don't need you messed up in this. I need a level head at the club. Make sure no booze is served at the club if we don't make it back to the truck. This shouldn't take more than a few minutes. Understand?"

"Yes sir." Billy wanted to ask what a few minutes actually meant to Hirsh, but decided to stay silent.

Edward and Hirsh got out of the truck and walked to the back entrance. Billy drove around the corner and turned off the motor. He quickly began to get cold. He hoped this wouldn't take too long.

* * *

There were no streetlamps. Edward could barely see where he was going. They approached the back door and Hirsh knocked. No answer. He waited a minute and knocked again. Hearing no one, Hirsh turned the knob and opened the door. Their first sight was of what appeared to be their order, stacked up against the wall.

"Password."

Hirsh, noting that the voice seemingly came from nowhere, remembered the password. "Early."

"Start loading the truck and I'll get Pete."

Just as Edward picked up the first crate, the lights blazed bright, and all they heard were clicks of weapons being cocked.

"Put your hands where we can see 'em or we'll blow your brains out."

Edward, blinded by the light, put the crate down, but as he tried to make his way to the door, it slammed shut.

"Ain't nobody going nowhere," one of the voices shouted.

His eyes adjusting, Edward could now see LeBeck, in handcuffs, and Hirsh with his hands up.

"You are both under arrest for violation of the Volstead Act."

Both Edward and Hirsh were searched and their guns confiscated. "I would advise you strongly not to move," one of the agents shouted with his gun pointed at Hirsh.

In one corner of the room Edward could see four men lined up against the wall, all handcuffed. LeBeck's employees, probably. One of the federal agents had a rifle pointed in their direction. While Edward was forcefully handcuffed, he looked at Hirsh. Hirsh glanced up and ever so slightly tilted his head in the direction of their truck.

No way he's saying to run, Edward thought. *We'd be shot before we made it three steps.* There was nothing they could do but comply with the cops. Hirsh knew that too. What was his boss trying to communicate?

Hirsh again directed his eyes toward the truck. Edward thought harder. At last, it clicked. Billy was in the truck, waiting. And any second, the agents would have all of them secure, and start widening their search.

Edward gave Hirsh a nod that thankfully the agents didn't see, but couldn't come up with a solution. His lone hope was that Billy was smart enough to figure it out on his own. If he did, the boy could flee the scene before the agents started searching outside the building.

"Listen officers," Hirsh said trying to stall for time, "We were just-"

"If I wasn't clear before, I'll say it now. Shut the fuck up," one of the officers yelled in Hirsh's direction.

Edward realized Hirsh was trying to stall for time. Edward took the lead and in a moment of clarity, fell to the ground moaning in 'pain.'

"What's your problem, old man?" one of the officers walked in Edward's direction.

"It's my back, suh. I can't stand up."

"I'm not gonna say this again. Get up or I'll shoot you right here," another agent said with his gun pointing in Edward's direction.

Edward, taking his time, struggled to his feet.

* * *

Billy was startled when the building's windows abruptly blazed with light but stayed put, though his heart pounded at the suddenness. Hirsh said to wait, and he would wait no matter what.

Moments rolled by. He could make out the building's loading dock but was too far away to hear or see what might be happening inside the building. And then he saw a man, a long rifle in his hands, turning the corner of the building. Not Hirsh, or Edward. It was a uniformed federal agent.

Frozen by a combination of fear and indecision, Billy watched the man look around. He didn't think he could be

seen inside the truck, but he ducked down behind the
steering column anyway. He waited a few seconds, but then
slowly peered above the dashboard, in time to see the man
walk back around the corner and heard shouting inside the
building.

The key was in the truck's ignition. Thankful that he
wouldn't have to waste time retrieving it from his jacket
pocket, he turned the key, praying the truck wouldn't make
too much noise. He put the truck into reverse and crept out
of sight down an alley that ran along the side of the building,
opposite the back entrance.

With the building's lights on, he could see one of the cops
through a window. Another cop walked outside. If Billy tried
to get away now, he was sure he would be seen. He waited,
and even in the cold, beads of sweat began forming on his
forehead. He watched the cop walk back inside. Billy stayed
put for a minute more to make sure he hadn't been seen. As
he sat there, looking out of the windshield, panic set in as he
watched two agents walk out with LeBeck, Hirsh, Edward,
and several other men, all in handcuffs.

It wouldn't be long before they started looking for
Hirsh's truck. As soon as the cops seemed distracted with
putting the men into various vehicles, he made his move.
Leaving the truck's headlamps off, he backed down the alley
until it connected with a side street. He pressed the brakes
and waited. He watched several cars drive by in the rearview
mirror, and continued to wait. He turned his head to look
through the windshield. Still, no one appeared at the other
end of the alley. They weren't looking for him. Yet.

He had no idea how long he waited. Seemed like a
lifetime. Sweat dripped into his eyes. The rain started again,

and became mixed with sleet, then with snow. He couldn't see as well now in either direction; ice had started to form on the windshield and back window. Before he couldn't see at all, he had to move.

But first, he had to know what he was moving to—for all he knew, cops could be waiting at the end of the alley to ambush him. He got out of the truck and walked down the alley to the side street. With snow still coming down, he stuck out his head just enough to look both ways. Seeing no cars stopped or looking suspicious, he returned to the truck, got back inside, shifted to drive, and eased up on the brake. At the side street he looked both ways again, then turned left and merged into light traffic.

He doubted the Feds would recognize the truck now—it was heavily dusted with snow—but stayed with the flow of traffic. When he neared the club he passed it, checking for anything that looked amiss. Seeing nothing out of the ordinary, he circled around and parked a block from the club, and made that last block on foot, snugging his jacket close to his chest and neck against blowing snow.

He entered through the back entrance, peeked around inside, saw no trouble, and made his way to the front.

"Where the fuck have you been?" George groaned from the bar, where he'd been sitting with his head on folded arms.

The restaurant held only about a dozen customers; all of them seemed occupied with the waiters. With three long, determined strides, Billy closed the distance between them. "Shut up. Can't you see we've got customers? Hirsh and Edward were arrested at LeBeck's."

George looked at him, slack-jawed. "You couldn't do nothin'?"

"No, I couldn't. Hirsh told me not to stick around if there was trouble. I had to wait and make sure they didn't follow me. I'm lucky I didn't get arrested too."

"Well what are we supposed to do now?"

"Hirsh said that if there was any trouble, to keep the club open and not to serve any booze."

George snorted a laugh. "That ain't much of a problem. We don't hardly have any."

Billy could tell he would have to keep the club running on his own. George wouldn't be any help. "No gambling either."

"I think I got that."

Billy waited until George's head had drifted back to his arms, then headed into the kitchen. "Bruno, all we got tonight is a dinner service. No booze or gambling. We ran into trouble at LeBeck's, and Hirsh and Edward are locked up. If anyone asks for booze, tell 'em we don't serve liquor. If they've been here before and insist, tell 'em we don't serve no more. It might hurt us in the short run, but we have no choice."

"I *weel* make fantastic dinners. No one *weel* miss the booze," Bruno said with confidence.

Billy couldn't help a grin. "Let's hope."

"What about that big party that's coming tonight?" Antonio reminded Billy.

"Do you have their telephone number?"

"No. But it must be written down here somewhere."

"Find it. Maybe they'll show for dinner and move on for the booze."

"Tell them Chef Bruno have excellent menu planned," Bruno happily chimed in.

"Good. You'll need it."

Billy took the elevator to the third floor. He cleared the room of any bottles, made sure the gaming room was secure, locked all entrance doors and then made his way back down to the restaurant. He pulled Chef Bruno aside.

"Ok. The third floor is locked tight. I'll keep an eye on the restaurant. Make sure the staff knows to deny any reference to the room upstairs." He paused for a moment, looking around the room. "And one more thing. We can't let George out of our sight tonight. Got it?"

"Ci. I don't know your troubles with George, but I *weel* make sure he causes no problems. You can count on Chef Bruno."

"Ok, let's hope for a quiet night."

Chapter 27

 Washington, DC, 2015

"Looks like a bunch of ... dollar figures?"

"It sure does," Clarence said. "Look at the bottom. Is that a total? Whew. A hundred and eighty-five thousand dollars? And look, there's other numbers beneath it. Do you think this is the money we're looking for?"

"It's a great start. But the money wasn't in the box."

Clarence was looking discouraged.

"Don't get discouraged on me now, Clarence. We have one more place to go. Let's head to Whispering Pines."

Clarence grabbed his coat and patted one of the pockets, making sure he had the map. Giving me "ok" sign, we hopped in the car and after a brief fifteen minute car ride, found ourselves near the old cemetery.

"Keep your eyes open. According to my GPS, the cemetery is around here somewhere." I had a hard time believing there was a cemetery this close DC, city limits.

"There it is," Clarence signaled as we drove right past it.

We drove around the cemetery a few times. Once convinced we were at the right place, I parked the car on the side of the road, and we walked toward the entrance. I was ecstatic that we didn't come at night. Even though I dug up stuff in creepy locations for a living, something about tombstones unnerved me.

We approached a short black metal fence that surrounded the cemetery and stood at the rusted gate. As I surveyed the area, it looked like the groundskeepers had taken the last few years off. Or maybe decades. Clarence took the map from his coat pocket. Despite our best efforts, the map didn't match anything in front of us, even when he turned the paper every which way, giving no help to locate a possible gravesite.

"Might as well just go in there and see if anything clicks," I said.

Clarence followed me through the rusted gate and we made a purposeful amble through rundown plots with tombstones crumbling from the weather. Weeds grew in every direction.

Walking to the back of the cemetery, there was a slight decline in the terrain. Among a few gravesites, I noticed one lone pine tree. Must have been the place's namesake I thought, and gave the map an idle look. What I'd forgotten: there was a tree marked on the paper!

Excited, I called Clarence over and we headed for the tree, but didn't see a gravesite, just rocks scattered about and a narrow creek within sight distance. I let my eyes linger on the tree, hoping to have an "'X' marks the spot" moment. No luck.

"This must be the area. I can feel it." Clarence looked at me for some type of affirmation.

"Well if it is," I said, "I'm not sure what we're supposed to find."

We surveyed the area a few more minutes. Not recognizing anything, except maybe the tree, we decided the drawing must have been a false lead designed to divert attention away from something else.

We walked back to the car, silent and mostly dejected. Both of us were hoping to find a pot of gold. But I guess that would've been too easy. We were plainly stalled. Instead of starting the car right away, I sat in the driver's seat and thought. Clarence sat silent, staring out of the window. It was time for an aggressive plan, and one formed more strongly in my mind the longer I sat.

"Here's what I think," I said when I felt ready to share. Clarence looked my way. "We need to go back and see Dorothy. Unless we're missing something, there's no way she could afford Fountain View on her limited salary. And I can't get it out of my head that she mentioned the key. She's got to be the missing link here."

Clarence shrugged. "I've thought that all along, but could never get her to talk. You had better luck, and 'cept for the key, that ain't sayin' much."

"Let's split up. I'll drop you off at the hotel. Work on getting another meeting with Dorothy. Also check with Hank to see if that guy's been snooping around the house again. And one more thing." I turned in the seat to face him.

"When you talk to Hank, tell him we might need a handyman. See if he might be available. I have a plan if Dorothy is conveniently unavailable. Upgrade your room to a two-room suite. Are you comfortable with this?"

"Yes I am, Miss Mel." Knowing that he was spending his retirement money, the determination in his eyes to finish this made my heart lurch. I had to find the money, if the money existed!

"I'm going back to the library and check out any news about the club in 1934. I didn't get that far in the research, and I keep feeling 1934 matters. I need to check in with my office too. Let's meet for dinner in the lobby at six."

"I like your thinkin'," Clarence said, and smiled.

I checked my voicemail and noticed that I had several calls from my office. What now?

I punched in Beverly's direct line. "What's up, Bev?"

"Well … there are a few things we need to discuss. Do you have a minute?"

"Shoot."

"Okay." Beverly rattled off requests for quotes from sites in Israel and the US. We discussed the hiring of her new assistant, and financial issues that needed my attention. Then she got to why she'd really called.

"So this guy stopped by yesterday. Didn't say his name, but he also asked for Clarence."

A chill went through me. "Did he leave his name?"

"No. But when I told him you weren't available, he didn't look too happy. He gave me the creeps."

"What did he look like?"

"Well …he looked normal enough. Tall and thin, maybe thirtyish, with blond hair. Nicely dressed. But it was his demeanor I didn't like."

"Did he say at all what he wanted?"

"He said he was following up on your request to have the floors redone."

A request that had never crossed my lips. "Beverly, here's what I want you to do. I believe I know who that is. I don't believe he's dangerous, but just to be on the safe side, I'd like you to work from home for the next week. We don't get that many visitors anyway. Take what you need and forward all calls to your phone. Don't return to the office until I say so. If you have to, keep the door locked while you're there. Can you do that?"

"Uh … sure. Okay. Mel, what's up?"

"I think he's somehow related to the case I'm working here in DC. I have no idea yet how he's related, but I feel we're getting close, or he wouldn't be trying to see me in person. I want you to take precautions. And do me a favor. You haven't met my daughter, but I'm going to give you the phone number. I'd like you to call her—her name's Abby. And stay in touch with her daily. I'll let her know you'll be calling."

"Are you okay?"

"I'm fine, Bev. Really I am. It never hurts to take precautions. Now pack up and head for home. I'll call again soon. Got it?"

"Yes, Mel. Be careful."

We said goodbye and I called Abby, feeling guilty when I realized I hadn't called her back. I got her voicemail.

Knowing she hated long, newsy messages more than I did, I simply asked her to call me.

Chapter 28

 *Washington, DC, 1933*

After a quiet night, George left for home and Billy locked the front door. Billy stayed at the club all that night and dozed off sometime in the early morning hours. He awoke at nine to the sound of a ringing phone.

"Mayflower Club."

"Finally," he heard Hirsh say. "Listen, this is my one phone call. I have an attorney in Arlington. His number's on my desk. Call him and get him over here, even if you have to drive him yourself. Don't take no for an answer. Tell him we've been arrested for booze. I'll tell him the rest when he gets here." Almost as an afterthought he asked, "How'd it go last night? Any problems?"

"Not a one. I'll be there with your attorney as quick as I can."

"Thanks, Billy," and with that the line went dead.

As Billy set the phone back into its cradle, George walked into the club. "Any news?"

"Hirsh wants me to pick up his attorney and take him to the jailhouse. Stay here, I'll be back as soon as I can."

"I don't take orders from you."

"Just stay here. Hirsh is counting on you. He said so on the call," Billy lied.

George sneered as Billy raced upstairs to get the phone number.

Billy came back downstairs to make the call. He got no answer. The address was on the paper, so he put the phone back under the bar and left in search of the attorney.

George watched Billy walk out the door. It was rare that he was alone in the club. He didn't have a key, though he'd sometimes asked Hirsh about it. A mere oversight, he thought.

George heard the telephone ring. Where did that Billy put that phone?

The rings were coming from under the bar? He finally found the phone and went to reach for it. As he did, he knocked his hand against the back brick wall, and it felt as though one of the bricks had moved. That was odd.

He put the phone on the bar and growled, "Mayflower Club."

The reply was fast, and bewildering. "Hey Billy, it's Edward. I'm callin' ya from the jailhouse. Hirsh was tryin' to get ahold of his lawyer. Were you able to reach him?"

George's head was buzzing, and the stomach acid trying to eat him alive wasn't helping his mood. "I ain't Billy, and we already talked to Hirsh. That's all I know." And with that, George hung up the phone.

As he returned the phone to the shelf underneath the bar, he looked again at the brick wall. He put his hand on one of the bricks and pushed; it seemed to move, if slightly. He tried to move the brick toward him, wiggled it back and forth. It finally came out, along with a few more. He couldn't see inside the small opening he'd created. Too dark. He reached his hand inside and thought he felt something solid. Cool, like metal. With both hands, he pulled out a metal box. There was a key lock but it wasn't locked; he opened it with ease.

Inside was a piece of paper, a key, and a load of cash. George had no idea how much cash, but it had to be tens of thousands of dollars. He stared at the cash a moment, then looked around the bar to make sure he was still alone. Seeing no one, he stowed the box under the bar and then hurried into the kitchen to find a bag. When he returned, he shoved the cash and the key into the bag, and in his excitement forgot about the piece of paper.

He put the box back into the space and carefully positioned the bricks the way they'd been, and picked up a rag and wiped the area under the bricks clean.

He returned to staring at the cash inside the open bag. He had no idea who it belonged to or where it came from. But it was his now. He quickly reasoned that it couldn't be traced back to him. George took a moment and surveyed the room once more to make sure he remained alone in the club. Satisfied his surroundings were secure, his paranoia dissipated, and he returned his focus to the money.

George removed one of the stacks from the bag. He counted $20,000. He fished through the bag and counted eight additional stacks and a few loose bills. Almost $185,000! More money than he could make in twenty years. He put the stack back into the bag, thinking. He couldn't leave the money in the club. Too risky. Since he didn't live far from the club, he'd take it home and stash it. The money must be part of the take from the club. But it couldn't be Hirsh's, he reasoned. Why would he hide his own money behind the bar?

George surveyed the area again. Without a key to the front door, he'd have to leave the club unlocked. He hopped into the car and on the short drive home, he stared out the windshield, thinking. Someone was stealing from the club. The only other person he reasoned with access to a large sum of money was Edward. There was no one else. But why hide it in the club? And why hide it behind the bar?

George opened the door to his house. He didn't hear anyone and decided to walk around the house to make sure he was alone. He knew he couldn't tell Cecilia. After all, she was Hirsh's daughter. Not to mention she was a lush and he didn't trust her. He needed to stash the money in a place his wife would never look.

He peeked into the bedroom and found Cecilia still passed out from last night's bender. He went into the spare bedroom, opened the closet, and pulled out his largest tackle box. He removed the fishing and hunting gear and replaced it with the cash, then hid the gear underneath the bed. He looked in the bag for the key but couldn't find it. He turned the bag inside out. Still no key. He looked around the room.

A quick search didn't reveal where it had gone, but he reasoned he must have dropped it somewhere in the house.

He had to get back to the club. He felt confident he'd stumble across the key later. He returned the fishing box to the closet, and hurried back to the club. In his haste, he failed to notice his daughter was watching his every move.

George arrived at the club and took a momentary glance upstairs and downstairs. He walked into the kitchen and, satisfied that no one was around, he walked behind the bar, bent down to make sure the bricks were in place and as he stood, he saw Antonio just arriving for work.

"Any news from Hirsh?" Antonio asked as he walked by the bar.

"Billy went to get Hirsh's lawyer. That's all I know."

* * *

Billy didn't know Arlington well and got lost several times. He finally saw the sign "Sindel Adecrombis, Attorney at Law." He found a convenient parking spot and hiked up the brick stairs to the entrance. He approached an ornamental glass door and noticed multicolored light prisms reflecting on the light brown floor as he opened the door.

"May I help you?" a disheveled looking receptionist asked in a rushed tone as he entered the office.

"Yes, I'm looking for Mr. Adecr ..."

"He's in court right now," she curtly replied, eyes on her typewriter.

"Could you give him a message for me? My name is Billy, and I'm here on behalf of Hirsh Rosenburg. He's in jail, you see, and he'd like Mr. Adecromie to meet him there."

She stopped typing and looked up. "That is a shame. Him being in jail and all. And it's Adecrombis. Mr. A-de-crombis," she pronounced each syllable. "I'll tell him when he gets back. Tell Mr. Rosenburg that Mr. Adecrombis is in court all day. It will have to be late tonight."

"Thank you, ma'am. I will ma'am. Have a nice day, ma'am," Billy said as he tipped his hat and searched for the doorknob behind him to exit the office.

Billy, dejected, walked back down the stairs and opened the door to his truck. He placed the keys into the ignition, but didn't crank it right away. He'd have to be the one to convey the unwelcome news to Hirsh. The news would not be well received, he was sure. He leaned his forehead on the steering wheel. What was he going to say?

After gathering enough courage to start the truck, Billy made the thirty-minute drive to the jailhouse. He arrived at the dilapidated red brick building and walked up to the entrance. Billy had never been to a jailhouse before. He'd never envisioned a circumstance that would find this visit necessary. He was an artist, not a lawbreaker. Upon brief reflection, however, he was now, an artist working at an illegal nightclub and if not careful, this jailhouse could be in his future too.

"Yes, young man, what can I do for you," a police officer said as he entered the door.

"I'd like to see Mr. Hirsh Rosenburg or Mr. Edward Higgins, if possible sir."

"Let me see what I can do."

The officer disappeared and Billy glanced around the office. After what happened last night, he realized he could also be behind bars at this very moment. Not a pleasant thought. He plopped down in one of two stained, thinly cushioned chairs. Sitting next to him, a man who smelled like rotten fish, slept against the wall. He hurriedly rose from the chair and decided that standing was the better option. He leaned against the front desk and, gazing out of the front window, hoped he wouldn't be there much longer.

Within a few minutes, the officer returned and asked Billy to follow him. Dutifully, he followed the officer into a dingy, dark room. After a time, Hirsh appeared, wearing handcuffs and looking frazzled and exhausted.

The officer removed the handcuffs and retreated to one corner. Billy looked up at the cop. Fairly sure he could hear everything said, he began speaking in a hushed tone.

"How are you?"

"Never mind that. Did you get my attorney?" Hirsh asked.

"I went by the office. He's in court all day. He should be here tonight. Are they going to offer bail?"

"Goddammit. I pay that guy a shitload of money to be available when I need him." Hirsh put his head in his hands. "I gotta be bailed out today. I need Sindel now. Not tonight. That son of a bitch."

Billy didn't know what to say, so he just sat there.

Hirsh looked up. "How's the club?"

"It's okay. Dinner went smoothly and everything else is good," Billy said, glancing up at the cop.

"Well at least one thing's going right."

There was silence for a moment, then Billy said, "What should I do with the receipts?"

"Well," Hirsh said in a quieter tone, and leaned in toward Billy, "open the closet in my office. You'll see a little safe. Count the money and write down the tally. Keep the paper to yourself. Do not tell George. Do you have a pencil?"

"No, but I'll remember."

Hirsh rattled off the numbers and Billy repeated them. The cop appeared to remain indifferent.

"Got it," Billy said. "Anything else I can do?"

"I expect to be out on bail by tomorrow. We'll talk then."

"Okay boss."

"Wait. One more thing. They did allow me to call Millie, but she wasn't at home. No need to mention this in case she comes by the restaurant."

"Yes boss. I'll let everyone know."

"You're a good kid, Billy. Thanks."

"Before I leave, how's Edward?"

"Feisty old goat. When I see him, I'll let him know you asked."

With that, Hirsh stood, and the cop put the handcuffs back on and they left. Billy sat there for a moment, stared around the room, and hoped he'd never be back again.

Chapter 29

 *Detroit, 2015*

Bev was able to book us on the six-thirty flight to Detroit. We had no idea if Hirsh's granddaughter Dorothy would meet with us again. She didn't return any of our calls.

"Let's try her one more time," Clarence said as he picked up the phone. After a few seconds I heard Clarence say, "I'd like to speak with Dorothy Clemmons please."

A few more seconds rolled by. "I'm sure you know my voice by now. Clarence Higgins," he put his hand over the phone and said, "they keep asking who's calling."

Barely a minute went by before Clarence hung up the phone without saying goodbye. "They said she was unavailable at the moment."

At that point, both of us knew Dorothy wasn't getting the messages.

"Well looks like we go with Plan B," I said in my most optimistic tone.

His eyebrows rose. "Care to share with me now, what this Plan B involves?"

"Call Hank. Tell him we need him tomorrow night. Here's what I'm thinking. And just listed for a minute. We need to remove Dorothy from the old folks' home." I let that sit for just a second, and seeing the astonished look on Clarence's face, I continued without interruption. "Look, we need her, and she won't see us. Or they won't let her see us, which I think is the case. Somehow I'd like to believe she wants out of that place. We're just helping the process along. I'm going on a sort of reconnaissance mission. Check the place out. Best if we both don't go. I've only been there once, so I don't think they'll recognize me."

Clarence still had that same astonished look. Probably not a good sign.

"Miss Mel, are you sure? I mean, I've agreed with your plans so far but this sounds … a little crazy."

I decided not to be deterred. Or waver in the slightest. "Call Hank. Let's meet tomorrow around noon. I'll have more information about the place by then. We can make a final decision, and I'll have Hank take a look at the place as well. If we all three agree, we take her from Fountain View tomorrow night."

"Miss Mel. I know what we've been doin' hasn't worked. And the money sure seems farther away than ever, but kidnapping? I don't know where to start. What if I just drop by, maybe she'll see me?"

"You can try, but they won't let her see you, take it to the bank. I need you to find Hank, get a meeting with him tonight. Let's just take it from there."

* * *

After an uneventful flight to Detroit, Clarence and I parted ways at the hotel. He barely spoke to me on our trip. Who could blame him? I was determined to put my plan in place, and Clarence thought I was nuts. Sure, what I wanted to do was risky, but I decided if I immersed myself in the planning stage, I wouldn't have time to see what a dicey plan I'd created. And my new criminal friend Hank would reassure me, I hoped.

The sun peering into my hotel was a signal to get moving. I dressed, bought a bagel and coffee from the hotel restaurant, and put-putted in my rental car to Fountain View. As I pulled into the parking lot, I looked up and down the long, narrow lot for light poles that might have cameras attached. There were ground-level lights in a few spots; I chose to believe they didn't hold cameras. So far so good. I noticed something I didn't on my first visit: a small park, on the side where I happened to be parked. Must have been for guests to use.

The parking lot was fairly full this time too, and being reasonably certain there were no cameras taping my every move, I decided to sit in the car, near the park, and take in the trees and grass. I took the bagel out of the bag, broke off a piece, and stared out the windshield.

Most of the residents' apartments faced the park. Each apartment had a small patio. I hadn't noticed that before. As I sat there, nibbling on my bagel with thoughts alternating between Jaimie and Clarence, I spotted movement in one of the apartments. Three people, exiting by way of the patio entrance. One might be dear Dorothy. Now I wished I'd brought binoculars. Had the trio come out of the third apartment from the street? Or maybe the fourth apartment? As I struggled for a better look, I was startled by a knock on my window.

A man I didn't recognize gave me the universal "roll down your window" sign. "May I help you, ma'am?" he politely asked.

Fortunately, I had a navigation unit in the car, and told him I'd stopped to look at my location, saw the park, and decided to spend a few minutes before heading on. Quick thinking.

"Where are you trying to go?" he said.

Didn't plan for that question just yet. "Oh, I've forgotten, the address is in my purse, I've got it right here ..." I grabbed my purse to stall for time, and looked around for anything to bail me out. I knew there was a hotel just down the street. I pulled out a piece of paper and looking at the note, pretended the name was written on the note.

"I'm meeting someone at the um ... Dunbar Hotel. I thought this was it. Must have passed it."

"If you exit this parking lot and turn to your right, it's about a half-mile down the road on the left."

"Oh, thank you. I don't know how I got so disoriented," I said, suggesting I was a bit of a ditz.

"Not a problem, but I'm going to have to ask you to move along. This parking lot is for residents and their guests."

"Oh, of course! And thank you." I faked a big grin.

As I closed the window, the man disappeared, and I was sure Dorothy had too. I assumed the guard was watching, waiting for me to leave. I shoved the note back in my purse and put the car in reverse, taking a last quick glance, and as luck would have it, I spotted Dorothy as she walked into the fourth apartment from the front. No cameras that I could see, and now I was reasonably sure which apartment was hers. With Hank's help, this ought to be a cakewalk.

I called Clarence from my hotel to tell him my mission was successful. He was obviously still not on board with the whole kidnapping idea. I reminded him that I believed we were removing Dorothy from a bad situation. I wasn't fully convinced of that myself, but needed to believe this to continue. I hoped he believed it as well.

Clarence confirmed that Hank could meet with us to discuss the details. The plan was in motion.

We would meet Hank in the hotel lobby at noon. Before our meeting, I called Abby.

"Where are you, Mom? I called you and never heard back!"

"I'm sorry sweetie. You know that's not like me. Are you worried about me—"

"Mom, some creepy guy was in the lobby of our apartment building and stopped me to ask about you. I'm afraid to leave the place alone."

Before she could continue I said, "Call Allen and have him come get you. Or you can call Steven. I don't think you're in any danger but ..."

"I already thought of that. Allen's staying here. What's going on? I got a call from Beverly too. She told me to stay put but wouldn't say why."

I drew in a breath, trying to think of a way to make her be cautious without terrifying her. "Honey … I think this is related to the case I'm working on. I don't think he's dangerous. Just trying to intimidate me. Keep Allen with you if you leave the building."

"Well since I have to walk Poodles, he's stuck here."

Poodles. I'd forgotten about my dog. Another responsibility I'd dumped on her. "I'm sorry," I said, and truly was. "Do you want me to come home?"

"No. Just get this case over with."

"You can always board Poodles."

"I may just do that if I see that creep again."

"Okay. Call me if you do see him again. I promise I'll answer quickly. I really am sorry. I love you."

"I know, Mom. And I'm fine. Just answer my calls."

"I'm sorry. Really I am."

I heard a sigh and, "Love you, Mom. Come home safe."

"I'll be home soon."

With that unfortunate exchange over, I took stock of what I was doing. Kidnapping, stealing. For what? Some money? For a guy I felt sympathy for but barely knew? And honestly, I wasn't sure there was any money.

I collapsed on my lumpy hotel bed. Lying there, staring at the ceiling, I took stock of this seemingly unsolvable caper that I bet Nancy Drew could have figured out by now. I thought back to when I first met Clarence. Seemed like forever ago. This was supposed to be a small, insignificant job, consulting a guy with a nutty, yet somewhat believable story. At the time, I believed I could help Clarence not only find a load of cash, but maybe, more importantly, legitimize his uncle's claim. Now I felt like I was in way over my head.

In painful reflection, I realized that I'd put myself in this position more than once. Living a status quo life was never enough for me. I'd chosen paths full of second guessing, stepping out of my comfort zone only to find myself landing in a pile of dog poop. And for what? The sake of challenging myself? Of boredom? Or selfishness? There's a time to challenge yourself, I thought, and another when good instincts tell you to back away. Forced to truthfully analyze my decisions, impulsiveness was winning. My own daughter seemingly said as much when I saw her in Australia.

I sat up and stared in the mirror. Feeling like I wanted to toss in the proverbial towel, I remembered Steven. The pillar of compromise in my life. I could have stayed in the relationship and found reasonable happiness. Was that so bad? Stability? Familiarity? And yes, Jaimie was a nice diversion, but I barely knew him and more importantly, he barely knew me, my life story, my kids, my family. I was getting too old to shake my life up with new people and uncomfortable situations. My life in LA was good. I had struggles, but I knew that life. For the first time I was just a teeny-tiny bit scared of all the change I, alone, had introduced into my life.

I got off the bed and took a long look in the mirror. I thought about the confidence Clarence had shown in me, about how Jaimie literally made me shiver. Like it or not, I needed shiver, uncertainty. I wasn't feeling strong about this declaration, more stating a fact. And in a small, sudden burst of clarity, I knew that the uncertain paths I chose to walk down were a part of me. I'd never really put much thought into all of this. Upon closer examination, it all sounded irresponsible, almost selfish. Why would I want to take a deeper look at these flawed traits? But quite possibly…this self-realization might be worth a second look. Maybe later.

Bringing the focus back to the problem at hand, I was on the verge of solving a real, modern mystery. This wasn't about bird bones or old clay pottery. Besides, Clarence believed in me, believed I could do it. After all the setbacks I'd had at my little archeology company, someone believed in me.

It was almost noon. I changed clothes, checked my phone. Seeing no calls from Jaimie, I headed downstairs.

Walking into the bar area, I saw Clarence and Hank at a table. Hank's demeanor was unreadable, but Clarence didn't look happy.

"Thank you for coming, Hank. Has Clarence mentioned my plan of attack to you?"

"I know some of the information," he looked at Clarence.

"Let me get right to the point. We have some unlawful breaking and entering to do again. Only this time instead of looking for a key, we need to kidnap an old lady."

Hank didn't look fazed. Which gave me confidence to continue.

"I'm not sure how much Clarence told you about his pressing family matters, but we're at a standstill, and I've decided to take an aggressive turn to hopefully move things along. Based on the key we stole and some paperwork I found, we believe that Hirsh Rosenburg's granddaughter, Dorothy Clemmons, is stonewalling us. And maybe, just maybe, it's because of something or someone pressuring her. So, even if we come up with a reason she'll believe, whatever *it* is will probably prevent her from coming away with us." I took a single deep breath. "So the best plan as I see it, is to forcibly remove her from Fountain View." I paused.

No questions or comments. Hank wasn't one to ask why, I confirmed. I continued.

"While I was casing the place this morning, a security guard asked me to move along. I didn't see a gun, but I can't be sure there wasn't one. We have to assume he, or someone, makes rounds twenty-four hours a day in a high-class place like that. There's only one level to the place, and a patio leads from each resident apartment to an open area or park. It looked like sliding glass doors separate the room from the patio. I can't be sure. We need to get from the parking lot, pass through three patios, each surrounded by a two-foot wall, and open a locked sliding door. Once we get inside the room, I need you to get Dorothy back to the car. I'll be looking around the room for anything I can find that might help us. What do you think you'll need?"

"Assuming the glass doors aren't wired, I need my pick lock, a crowbar, chloroform, and a glass cutter. We gotta assume there's a bar that prevents the door from sliding open. Worst case, I need to cut the glass. Otherwise, sounds fairly straightforward."

"Straightforward" didn't equate to "chloroform" in my mind. "About the chloroform? I don't know anything about chloroform."

Clarence didn't seem comfortable with the discussion. He said nothing.

"I can chloroform her, which'll keep her quiet for a little bit," Hank explained matter of fact. "What's your plan after we take her?"

"Sleeping pills, maybe? We just need to get her to Washington, DC, an eight-hour drive. I need you to go with us. I'll get you a hotel and pay for your return ticket to Detroit." I didn't clear this with Clarence, but at this point, if he balked, I'd be willing to do this on my dime. We needed Hank.

Hank shrugged. "Aw'right then. We got a plan."

"Obviously, I didn't pack any of the items you need in my suitcase. Guess we have some shopping to do. I have no idea where to find—"

"Don't worry. I got a source. You got money?"

"I'll get some."

"Good. If what you tellin' me is the truth, should be easy. When are we lookin' at takin' the old lady?"

"I'd like you to drive there after our meeting. There's a big office building across the street. You might be able to stay there for a while without being noticed. See if the guard has any kind of schedule. If it all looks good to you, we need to be ready for tonight. Can you get—"

"The tools are not a problem. You guys sure about this?" Hank said, looking more at Clarence than me.

"Look Hank, it's not like either of us has done this sort of thing before. It's why we called you. If you're not on board, tell me now."

"Don't worry about me. I just hope you and Clarence have a plan for after we take the old lady." He paused for a moment. "Guess that's not my problem. Get me the money and I'll get what we need."

I glanced toward Clarence. I realized he would be just as guilty if we were caught. Too late to worry about that now. Well, not technically. We could still call it off. But I didn't think Clarence would, and I knew I didn't want to. I glanced his way again and saw his nod, and felt relieved. By the end of tonight, either we were going to be one step closer to the money and the truth, or be in a heap of trouble.

Chapter 30

Washington, DC, 1933

"Where the fuck have you been?" Hirsh's temper on full display.

"Look, how was I supposed to know you'd gotten yourself in trouble again?" Sindel sounded almost irritated. "Left court as soon as I could. What's the charge?"

"Liquor violation. We were at LeBeck's buying booze." He pulled Sindel closer and whispered, "They still don't know about the games. Liquor only. Fortunately we were low at the time, and Billy got rid of the bottles at the club. Edward's here too."

Sindel nodded. "Yeah. I saw him first. Bail is low. I can get you out, but it won't be until morning."

"Shit."

"You're lucky I can get you out at all. They think gambling is going on."

"I told them," Hirsh said loudly, "that I wasn't involved in no gambling."

"Well, I would imagine that reassured them," Sindel said in a cynical tone. "I'll post bail for you and Edward tomorrow. Pay me back when we get to the club. I'll be here first thing."

"Could you check on the club for me? I don't trust no one there. Dinner is on the house. Stay until closing. They ain't supposed to have any liquor, but just want to be sure."

Sindel nodded. "I'll do it. This one's going to be tough to get out of. You know that. The Mayflower Club is too visible."

"I've got some strings I can pull. Political strings. Just get me out. I'll worry about the club."

"See you tomorrow."

"Could you let Edward know on your way out?"

With a heavy sigh, Sindel nodded.

* * *

Sindel arrived at the jailhouse bright and early in the morning, paid the bail, and drove Edward and Hirsh to the club. On the drive, Hirsh thought about his next step, decided his first call would be to Senator Hughes. Someone had to be paid off. The senator would know who to bribe.

"How'd it go last night?" Edward asked Sindel.

"It was slow," Sindel said. "But without booze, only a few people stayed for dinner. I talked to Billy, and we closed the place by nine."

Hearing this, Hirsh winced. "It won't be long before we're back in business."

"It should be. The club is toxic right now. Unless you like jail time."

"I told you. I got connections," Hirsh said, annoyed.

"I don't want to hear about any connections. My advice is to stay clear of the booze and gambling for a while."

"I'd expect that advice from you, but it ain't happenin'. Just be easier to reach, will ya?"

Sindel pulled in front of the Mayflower Club. "Unless I'm in court, I'll call right back. And I'll stop by later for the money. Just try and remember what I said."

Hirsh simply closed the car door.

Before they walked into the club, Hirsh pulled Edward aside. "We're startin' back up in a few days."

"I figured as much, boss. I know there ain't no changin' your mind."

"No there ain't. We just need to be a bit more careful, like Sindel said. I'm calling the senator. Should keep the heat off for a time."

What other response could there be? Edward simply nodded.

"Welcome back," Billy said to Hirsh as soon as he saw him.

"Glad to be outta there. I hear it's been quiet here."

"As a church mouse."

"Well, that's about to stop." Hirsh patted Billy on the back. "Let's meet on the third floor in a few minutes. I need a drink."

As Hirsh walked upstairs, Billy said, "He's in a good mood."

"I'm not sure why," Edward responded with his eyes fixed on the parquet floor.

Billy climbed the stairs to the second floor, went to the elevator, and pushed the button to the third floor.

Downstairs, Edward looked around the restaurant area of the club until he remembered he'd forgotten to lock the cashbox. He went behind the bar, loosened the bricks. He grabbed the box and pulled it out, and almost dropped it. It felt different. Light.

"Shit," he muttered. He opened the box. The cash was gone. All of it. He felt instant sweat beads on his forehead, and then dizziness. He shoved the box back into the space and replaced the bricks. Only he and Hirsh knew about the box. He was sure of that. Who'd been at the club alone while he and Hirsh were in jail? George, Antonio, Billy?

There was no explaining this to Hirsh. He wouldn't understand that their stash of money was missing. He'd demand an explanation, the same one Edward's mind was desperately trying to come up with. He made his way to the third floor. Only Billy was in the room.

"While we were away, was anyone left alone in the club?" Edward tried to sound casual.

"No, there's always a few people here ..." Billy thought again. "Except when I had to leave to get that attorney."

"Who was here then?"

"George. I had to leave him in charge, no one else was here."

"By himself?"

"I think so. No, I'm sure of it. Why?"

Hirsh walked into the room and started talking to Billy. Edward couldn't think, couldn't hear.

"Did you hear me, Edward?"

Edward snapped his head around to look at Hirsh. "I'm sorry, what boss?"

"I said, we'll stay clean tonight, but we'll be fine to start back up tomorrow night. I'm picking up the booze tonight from ... a different distributor. I expect no trouble, but best not to mention names anymore. You two are in charge while I'm away. By the way, either of you guys seen George?"

"Not this morning, boss," Billy said.

Edward tried to listen as Hirsh rattled off more instructions, but all he could think about was the missing money. The meeting ended and Hirsh headed towards the elevator.

Edward looked at Billy, "I've got to run an errand. I'll be back in a few minutes. Could you handle whatever Hirsh said he needed?"

Billy simply nodded.

Thank God Billy heard Hirsh's rambling instructions. He grabbed his coat and the keys for the truck, still not quite sure what to do. He had no definitive proof that George took the money. But who else could have taken it? That firmed up his decision about his next destination.

Edward walked to the back alley where the truck was parked. He didn't like to drive, but the sooner he got to George's house the better. He put the key in the ignition, cranked the motor and pulled away from the club.

After the short drive and no real plan, Edward pulled up to George's house and looked around. No one on the street, no meddlesome neighbors looking out their windows that he observed. He got out of the truck and walked to the fence that surrounded George's yard. He looked alongside the house to the backyard. Not a soul in sight. He walked to the front door and knocked. He put his ear to the door. Hearing nothing, he tried the knob, not expecting it to turn, and the door opened.

Chapter 31

 *Detroit, 2015*

Clarence called me in the late afternoon with details of Hank's reconnaissance mission. "He didn't provide many details," he told me, "but he still thinks the job should be relatively easy."

Feeling reassured, we planned to meet that night at eleven thirty in the parking lot across the street from Fountain View.

Clarence supplied Hank with the cash he needed to buy the tools. I spent the afternoon researching chloroform and its effects. There were risks, especially with the elderly, but we needed just enough to get her to the car, and then supply her with a few sleeping pills to keep her sleepy for eight hours.

At eleven p.m., Clarence and I left the hotel for our rendezvous site. At exactly eleven thirty we met Hank across the street from Fountain View. With too much time on my hands to think, I needed to clear up a few details. "So Hank, what's our plan to avoid the security guard?"

Hank looked at me. "Don't worry about minor details. Even though you look stunning in your black kidnapping attire," he gave me a curt smile, "I'm going in alone. You and Clarence are staying here. I know what I'm doin' and I don't need two rookies screwin' it up."

Somehow, I was offended by this. As well as being scared shitless. I tried not to let it show, but I know it must have. Clarence's expression told me he was too. We both quietly listened to Hank.

"There are cameras," he heard my gasp but gave a dismissive wave of his hand. "Only on two of the light poles. And they're at the front of the building. The guard doesn't stay outside the premises the entire time. Every hour for about ten minutes, he goes inside. Not well thought-out, but good for us. This is gonna be one of my easier gigs."

Although Hank might have had a point about the rookie stuff, I'd dressed up for this caper and I insisted on going along. I tried reason. "Look, you've never seen Dorothy before. And we aren't sure exactly where she'll be. Besides, I need to look around her room while you're doing what you'll do. Clarence is staying here, sure, but I'm going with you. End of story. Let's go."

Maybe it was my forceful tone. Maybe I made some sense. Hank thought for a moment and after a pensive look in my direction, surprisingly, he relented. "Okay, but when I say we're leavin' the room, we're leaving. Got it?"

"I got it."

Hank started in on the details. "Clarence, this should take ten minutes tops. Three minutes to the room, two minutes in the room and three minutes back. That leaves us a couple extra minutes in case of problems. I need you to drive the car away from the area, just in case. Be back in eight minutes. If more than eleven minutes go by and you don't see us, assume there's trouble. No sense in you gettin' caught, too."

"What should I do if you get caught?" Clarence said.

I pulled my notebook and a pen from my purse. "This is Jaimie's number. Call him. I'll be in touch with Jaimie somehow if this goes wrong. Then we can take it from there."

Clarence took the note. His former tendency to panic wasn't present. He seemed rather confident, actually. Which calmed me.

"Ready?" Hank looked in my direction.

"Ready."

"Follow directly behind me. Don't look up. Look where you're going. Can't afford to have you trip. You'd be surprised how often that happens."

How many times had Hank pulled a caper like this, I wondered. Maybe the more the better? Better not to know? I chose the latter.

I followed instructions, noting how quiet the night was. We ran toward the right of the building. Before I knew it, we were at the solid wall that divided the parking lot from the back of the rooms. We both easily hopped the wall. Hank breezed by the first room and waved me forward, but stopped just before the second set of sliding doors.

"What's wrong?" I whispered.

"Some kinda nurse in the room and the light's on."

In the back of my mind, I was thinking about the eight minutes. Time was ticking. What would we do with a drugged old lady and no driver?

Hank grabbed my arm. I looked at my watch and another minute went by. Hank risked another look into the room.

"The nurse has her back turned. I'm going for it. Stay here until I get to the third room."

"Then what?" I said, waiting for specific instructions.

"I'll wave you forward if she didn't spot me." Which left unsaid that if she saw him pass the doors, I should run.

Without being noticed, he made it to the third room. He peered into the room and waved me forward. "Run to me," the hand said. I held my breath and ran.

Dorothy was in the fourth room. I was fairly sure about that. But four minutes had gone by and we weren't inside yet.

We reached the fourth room to find its curtain closed. Hank took out his burglary tools and went to work on the door. We were inside within a few seconds.

The room was dark, but with just enough light to confirm it was Dorothy. While he put her to sleep, I looked around the room for something, anything that might help Clarence's case. I saw a desk and started opening drawers, pulled out a penlight and shuffled through papers.

"Time to go," came the whisper.

"But I—"

"Let's go."

I saw Dorothy in his arms.

As I closed the last drawer, Hank opened the curtain. The moon provided a faint light on the desk, and the small maroon book on top of the desk. I grabbed it and followed Hank out the glass door. Six minutes.

We made it to the third room and passed those doors without incident, and stopped at the second room.

Hank, beginning to waver under Dorothy's weight, looked at me. "See if we can make it."

By that time, I was feeling confident. I could do this. I peeked into the room. The nurse was still in there.

"Okay," Hank whispered my way, "when she turns her back, you need to go and meet Clarence."

"What about you and, well … her?"

"We'll get there. Don't look back. Just go. Wait five minutes and if I'm not there, take off. Got it?"

"Five minutes. Got it." I looked at my watch.

I peered into the room again. The nurse was facing toward me. Her gaze was elsewhere—she hadn't spotted me—but just the same I jerked my head back and looked at Hank. Dorothy had to be getting heavy. How was he going to run with her? He was the pro here, I reminded myself, and turned back to the room's door for another peek. The nurse had her back to us now. I took off, passing the first room, then hopping the wall and racing toward the parking lot.

I never looked back. But I forgot the advice about looking down. Halfway through the parking lot, I tripped on one of the blocks placed to keep drivers from overshooting their space. I hit the ground hard, but my knee took the brunt. Dazed, I felt someone touch my shoulder. In a panic, I turned over and looked up.

"Told you to look where you're going," Hank said with a smirk.

He shifted poor Dorothy's weight and held out his hand to help me up.

"You can make it the rest of the way," he instructed. And I chose to believe him.

Me hobbling, we made it to the street, and Clarence opened the car door as soon as he saw us approach. Just short of eleven minutes.

Hank gently placed Dorothy in the back seat and I slid in after her. We eased closed the doors, and as Clarence drove down the dark street, I got my first real glance at Dorothy.

I tapped Hank's shoulder. He turned around. "Hank, I think she's dead."

"You just never seen anyone chloroformed," Hank assured me, "Dorothy's fine." Having a dead person on my conscience, even if she was old, would probably have been more than I could take just then.

It was a long eight-hour drive to Washington, DC. Between the sleeping pills and chloroform, Dorothy slept the entire trip. I tried to doze off, but my knee throbbed. I reached for my purse looking for anything for the pain. No luck.

We arrived at the hotel, and Hank instructed Clarence to drive around to the side. He took my key, unlocked the side door, and accepted Clarence's help to get Dorothy up the elevator and inside our room.

"What do we do now?" I asked him.

"Wait for her to wake up."

"How long will that take, do you think?" I said, showing my lack of chloroform-followed-by-sleeping pill knowledge.

"It could take an hour, maybe less."

I needed coffee. "Clarence, she knows you. Best if you stick around and be here when she wakes up. I'm going to step out for a few minutes. I'll bring coffee."

As I walked toward the hotel entrance, I decided to call Jaimie. I'd just stepped outside when he answered.

"You what?" Jaimie shouted in the phone. "Look, I don't have to tell you that what you did was crossing the line and—

"Jaimie, I need you to be calm for me. I realize we … slightly broke the law—"

"There's no slightly breaking the law. Either you do or don't."

"Okay, we broke the law. But there was no alternative. We're close and I know she's the key. Knows about the key."

"Where is she now?"

I told Jaimie we had her safely in the hotel room and said, "We hope that when she wakes up, we can shake her down for information."

"Shake her down for …" Jaimie said, his disgust clear. "You're already talking like a criminal."

"If we can show her we're on her side, I think she'll help us. She has to. We have no choice. While we were kidnap— taking her out of there, I saw a book on her desk and took it with us. It looks like a bankbook. There's a starting amount of $185,000. Then there's a bunch of figures that don't make any sense."

"Sounds like you've got this all wrapped up," Jaimie said, his words biting with disbelief.

I remained silent.

"Look Melinda, I'm not trying to be sarcastic. Or maybe I am. You're closer to this whole situation than I am. Let me help."

"Just listen. I'm okay. I feel like we're close to solving this."

His chuckle relieved me. "I won't doubt you. Call me once you've spoken to her. Let's see what she says and go from there."

More silence while I realized he was right. What was I thinking, kidnapping? Breaking and entering? Who knows what else I was now guilty of committing?

"I'm confident, Jaimie. I'm confident we'll get information out of her. Just not sure what we'll do with her after that."

"Mel, I'm on your side. I worry about you. I think you're a bit impulsive, but maybe that's what I lo— like most about you."

My mind was too rattled understand the implication of what Jaimie just said. Sounded almost like love. But maybe I was delirious.

Boy, did I need coffee. "Go back to sleep. I'll call you later," I said, slightly peeved.

Chapter 32

Washington, DC, 1934

Edward eased open the door and called George's name. No response.

"George?" he called again. "Anybody? Hello?" Nothing. He stepped inside the house and had no idea what to do next. Still deciding, his feet took him to the kitchen.

He saw a door that might be to a pantry. Where do people store things? A pantry or closet. Edward opened the door, halfway hoping to see a bag or a box with cash sticking out of it. As he was rummaging through the pantry he noticed a tiny key on the floor. He picked it up, and noted the "s" on it. The key he'd kept in the cashbox. Certain confirmation that George had taken the money.

He placed the key in his pants' pocket, spotted a large paper bag and while reaching to grab it, felt the barrel of a gun against his neck.

"What the hell are you doing in my house?" George shouted.

"Where's the money, George?"

"Money. What money?"

Trusting that George wouldn't be brave enough to shoot, Edward slowly turned around. "You know what I'm talkin' about. Where'd you hide money? The money that was stashed in the box under the bar. You were the only one left alone at the club. I know you have it."

"I don't have to tell you shit. I'm the one with the gun in my hand. You're in my house. I could shoot you right now, and who would care about a dead Negro found robbing me."

Edward knew he was right. He also knew George was stupid and greedy. He needed to buy some time.

"Look George, Hirsh and I agreed to subtract a percent of the nightly profit and hide it. If the club was ever raided, we'd have a stash no one knew about. Our own insurance money."

"You're full of shit and trying to cover your ass. You took this money for yourself."

"If you don't believe me, ask Hirsh. And then explain to him why you stole his money from his club."

As George gave that a moment's thought, Edward decided it was his chance to take advantage, and he grabbed the gun from George. Bellowing, George tried to wrestle it from Edward's grip. Edward thought he heard a door close, but in this, the fight for his very life, he had no time to wonder about it. As they struggled, the gun went off, and the men fell apart.

Edward looked down and saw George bleeding from the neck. It seemed like blood was everywhere. He'd never seen a dead man before, but there was no question that George was, indeed, dead.

Edward scrabbled in the pantry and, not finding the money, he went to the bathroom on a search for towels. He ran back to the kitchen, tied a towel around George's neck to stop the bleeding, and did his best to clean up. Then he remembered hearing a door close. He went room to room, making sure no one was in the house. He saw no one.

In a bedroom, he saw an old quilt spread at the foot of a bed. He took it with him to the kitchen, wrapped George up in it, and finished cleaning the floor. He picked up the paper bag. No money in it.

"Shit," Edward said aloud. There was no time to keep looking. He thought about leaving George there, blood beginning to seep through the towel. But in a last-minute decision, he knew no one would believe his story if he was caught. He'd shot George in his own house. A death sentence for him. A white jury would find him guilty before the trial began. He needed to get the body out of the house, get away from here. Not by the front door either.

He went to the kitchen window. There was a narrow alley behind the house, and a frenzied glance told him there were no windows on any of the surrounding buildings. Edward looked out the kitchen door, saw no one, and drove the truck around to the alley. He parked the truck and went back inside to get George's body.

He knew of a small cemetery, only a few blocks away and fairly isolated. Ironically, no one would ever think to look for George there, of that he was certain. He tried to pick George up, but couldn't lift his dead body off the floor. He found a blanket inside a closet and placed the blanket underneath George and little by little, sliding him back and forth, dragged him to the back door. Struggling, and with all his might, he loaded the body into the truck, and hurriedly disguised it among some pieces of broken liquor crates. He went back into the house to make sure he'd left no evidence of him being in the house. There were blood stains on the floor, but they'd have to stay there. Satisfied with his efforts, he left through the back door and climbed in the truck.

He pulled up to the cemetery and after a quick look around, didn't see cars or people. He drove around until he saw a secluded spot next to a pine tree. He went to the back of the truck, pulled George's body out, and dragged it to the tree. Leaving him out in the open wasn't a wise choice. He grabbed branches from one of the few trees in the area and gathered dead leaves to cover the body. He didn't have a shovel in the truck, so he'd have to wait until later to put George in the ground.

Edward stared at the slight mound. He'd never killed a man before. He felt remorse. Not for George. He felt nothing for George. He had just killed a man, dragged him to a crude location, covered him with dirt, branches, and leaves, and was about to leave him unceremoniously in a trash heap. He continued to stare at the mound. He put his hands together in prayer. He didn't pray for George's soul. He decidedly prayed for his own.

Chapter 33

Washington, DC, 2015

By the time I returned to the room Dorothy was awake. She looked confused and slightly shaken up, but not as bad I thought she might be.

"This was a little drastic don't you think, Clarence? Where am I?" Dorothy was lightly shaking her head.

"You're in Washington, DC," he replied. "Look Dorothy, I have no intention of hurting you. I called you dozens of times, and they kept tellin' me you weren't available. Left a message every time. Didn't you get any of 'em?"

Dorothy ignored the question. "You know I have every right to call the police right now."

I knew this moment would come and I was prepared. "Oh, you could," I said. "But the police will ask questions, just like we are. We found a book in your room that lists an initial sum of $185,000. We've found this amount on other documents-"

Clarence held up a hand. "Easy, Miss Mel." Somehow, without a plan, we turned the situation into a good cop, bad cop scene. Then he returned his eyes to hers. "Miss Dorothy, we know that my uncle was stashing money in the club. I don't know how you got it, but if you don't have it, I believe you know where it is. When we came to visit you, you mentioned a key. We have that key—"

"I believe you hated Fountain View," I said. I decided I needed to stay assertive, to lay some assumptions on her. "It felt like a prison there. A nice prison, but a prison all the same. The German guy was overbearing, there were cameras everywhere, and security guards surrounded the place. There was some kind of deal between them and you. I'm not trying to justify taking you in the middle of the night, but I wouldn't have done it, if I felt you were happy there. Were you … happy there?"

She kept her face impassive. "Let me think on this for a minute. My head is still swimming from whatever you gave me."

"Only a sleeping pill. It'll wear off."

"I'll go get us some food," Hank offered. "That might help you, ma'am."

"Thanks, Hank," I said. "There's food at the bar downstairs." I turned my gaze back to Dorothy. "Taking you from Fountain View was my idea. Please don't blame Clarence."

She looked up at me, indignant. "Why am I not surprised by that?"

"I believed you were held at Fountain View as somewhat of a hostage, or at the very least you were miserable there. Is that true?"

No reply. I continued hoping I was onto something.

"There's been a man pursuing Clarence and me. I believe I briefly saw him at Fountain View. A few nights ago, we followed him to his house, and we found a key that he'd stolen from Clarence's house. We also found a cashbox hidden in the restaurant where the Mayflower Club was located. The key opened the cashbox, and we found piece of paper that mentioned $185,000. Is any of this making sense to you?"

Still silence, but I thought I saw her composure cracking, if only a bit. "We think that you—"

"What did the man look like?"

I didn't expect the question, so had to think a moment. "Blond. About six feet tall. Thin. And he had some sort of tattoo on the back of his neck."

For the first time, Dorothy's face showed recognition.

"We took a book from your room, and it mentions $185,000 dollars. And as I mentioned we also found that same sum on a piece of paper, in a box hidden in what was the old Mayflower Club. Too much of a coincidence, Dorothy."

I waited. And waited. The woman's face had returned to stone, and this time the state seemed permanent.

Chapter 34

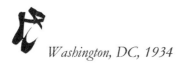 *Washington, DC, 1934*

"Where is it?" Cecilia shouted at her daughter.

"Where's wh—" before Dottie could finish, her mother, in a drunken stupor, slapped her.

"Where's the money you little bitch? You know where your precious daddy stashed it, he told you everything he did!"

"I don't know what you mean," Dottie replied with tears streaming down her face. But the tears were only because the slap had stung. "What money, Momma?"

"You know your daddy's dead. Not that I give a shit, but I heard him arguing with Edward about money. You *have* to know where it is."

"No ma'am, I'm sorry. I don't know where any money is."

Cecilia, seeing that threats and slaps weren't getting her what she wanted, took Dottie by the hand and led her into the living room. She sat her on the couch, gave her a tissue for her tears, and while holding her hand said, "Look honey, we could use that money. Actually, we really need it." She omitted that the "need" would come when Hirsh's patience and liquor ran out and Cecilia had to start buying her own booze. But a need was a need.

Sniffling with emotion as fake as her daughter's, she continued. "Honey, you know that Daddy worked hard at the club. Who's going to take care of us now if we don't have that money?"

"I truly wish I could help you, Momma, but honest, I don't know anything about no money."

"Okay sweetie, here's what I need you to do." The grip on Dottie's hand tightened. "You think about it. Think hard. Remember that money could be our ticket outta here. We could go somewhere new. Just me and you. If I had that money and didn't have to work, I might find the time to take you to those dancing lessons you're always yapping about. Wouldn't that be nice?"

Dottie wondered how her mother could make dancing lessons sound so unappealing. She considered her options, and her reply. At last she said, "All right, Momma, I will think about it. But I really don't know anything about any missing money."

Cecilia looked at her daughter. Looked at her hard. She still wasn't convinced, but it was useless right now to keep on. Best she looked around for the money herself. Not that she cared who'd killed George, but she knew Edward had no idea where the money was; her only mission now was to find it. Edward might come back with the same mission in mind.

"Listen young lady, you find any money, it's mine. You wouldn't know what to do with it. We're like partners now. Okay?"

"Yes ma'am."

"I've got to run to the store to get us dinner. You'll be okay. And think about that money while I'm gone."

Dottie went back to her room, which was now missing her favorite quilt. And now her daddy was gone forever. She'd heard the gunshot. The loud noise startled her. She'd heard Edward searching the house, too, quiet-like. She lay on her bed and thought what to do next. She wasn't giving the money to Mr. Edward, and she surely wasn't giving it to her mother, knowing her mother would only spend it on more drink. But Momma was right about one thing. What could a kid do with that much money?

* * *

After Edward left the cemetery, he walked aimlessly for hours. He'd killed a man, lost all Hirsh's money and, after running several scenarios through his head, had no idea how'd he explain this to anyone. He returned to his house, found a shovel and made the short walk back to the cemetery to put George in the ground. It was early afternoon before he returned to the club.

"Where's the boss?" Edward snapped at Billy.

"Where have you been? And where's George? Hirsh is flippin' out."

Edward wasn't in the mood to entertain questions, but only to have them answered. "Where is he?"

"Upstairs, I guess."

Edward took the stairs to the second floor, dreading every step closer to Hirsh's office, knowing that Hirsh would accuse him of stealing the money. Approaching the front door, Edward heard Hirsh on the phone. He waited and listened.

"Look, the money is stashed. Don't worry. I got it covered."

Then silence.

Edward heard, "On his way back from Spades. I got the whole thing worked out. Shot in that part of town? No one'll give a shit. And he's the only other one who knows where the money is."

Edward felt the cold tickle of beading sweat on his neck. As quietly as possible, he backed away from the door, mind racing. Had Hirsh been going to take the money all along?

He had to think. He'd killed a man for that money. For his loyalty to Hirsh. For their partnership. He thought back to when they had opened the club not that very long ago. He'd planned to steal from the club, to take what he believed was rightfully his. What had been denied to him all those years with Hirsh. But in the end, he couldn't do it. He just couldn't follow though. He wasn't a thief, a murderer. And now, hearing Hirsh on the phone, he was on his own. There was no partnership. He wasn't Hirsh's right-hand man. Had it been this way all along? For the past twelve years? He had no idea who Hirsh was talking to. But the message was clear. If he didn't move fast, he could be a dead man too. He headed back down the stairs.

"Where you goin'?" Billy asked.

Giving no response, Edward walked past him and out the front entrance, climbed into the truck, and drove to George's house. He thought about Hirsh on the short drive. It wasn't Hirsh who betrayed him. It was the club. The Mayflower Club. The dreaded Mayflower Club and all its pretentious, rich customers. He and Hirsh didn't belong to that crowd. They were back-alley, bathtub-gin types. Hirsh wanted to be a part of a crowd where he didn't belong. They should've never opened a joint on Connecticut Avenue. He didn't blame Hirsh. And he refused to believe that the only person on the planet who surely believed in him, who *needed* him, now wanted him dead.

Edward pulled up to George's house. The money had to be there. Maybe if he found it, took it to Hirsh, and replaced it, maybe he could win Hirsh back. Maybe.

Dottie was peering out the window when Mr. Edward approached, but drew back and hid when she saw him. She wasn't afraid of him. He seemed like a nice man. This was all her mommy and daddy's fault, not his. She went back to her hiding space.

At the door, Edward hesitated. The house looked empty, but he couldn't be sure. And he'd been wrong about that before, with deadly consequences.

He continued to stand there for a while, but no one came to the door. On the strength of that, he approached and knocked. No one answered. He knocked again. Hearing nothing for the next several seconds, he turned the doorknob. As before, no resistance. But a little girl was listening.

Inside the house, he called for George, knowing he wasn't there but wanting to find out if anyone else was. No answer.

Only then did he begin to search the house. He'd kept his emotions in check, but was in a panic now. The money had to be here, but a search of every room and closet, and even the crawl space, no money. He found a gun in one closet, and took it.

Though he'd covered the entire house, there was one thing he didn't find. Dottie remained one step ahead of him, had watched him search, with the confidence of knowing the money was in a safe place that Edward would never find.

Chapter 35

 *Washington, DC, 1934*

"Dottie, honey, you and I have to run an errand today. I need you to get dressed. We're leaving in a few minutes."

"Yes, Momma."

Dottie washed her face, put on her red-and-white polka dot dress, brushed her hair, put on her winter coat and mittens, and walked out to the car where her mom waited, puffs of mist coming out of its tailpipe.

As Dottie got into the car, she noticed her mom had been crying. "What's wrong, Momma?"

"Oh sweet darling, it's just been a tough morning."

Dottie looked toward the windshield and stayed quiet, and once they were driving, decided the windshield was still the best place to look.

They'd only driven for a few minutes when Cecilia parked the car in a field that was surrounded by woods. The snow had made the woods look really pretty. Dottie kept her eyes on them while she asked, "Where are we?"

"You'll see soon, darling."

They walked toward the part of the wooded area surrounded by a gate that was shorter than Dottie was tall. They stopped in front of a pile of dirt that looked freshly overturned. Only a little frost was showing on the clods of dirt.

"Darling," Cecilia said, "this is where your daddy is buried. I followed Edward here and watched him bury him. Your father was many things, but I did love him." Trying to judge her reaction, Cecilia looked toward Dottie. "I wanted you to see that he is really dead, and we are truly on our own."

Dottie walked a little closer to what she now knew was her daddy's grave. She didn't need to come here. She'd seen the fight, heard the gunshot. She knew her daddy was dead. And as far as she was concerned, it was all her daddy's fault. He was a lousy father, who never could stop Momma from drinking until she passed out. She looked up at her mother. She'd never stopped him from her daddy's abuse. Momma was a lousy mother too.

Unaware of her daughter's thoughts, Cecilia fixed Dottie with a pleading look. "So you see, honey, we could really use that money. You know I can't work and without it, we could be homeless. Do you want that?"

Dottie had no idea why her mother couldn't work. And she didn't care. She'd had a long time to think before she finally fell asleep last night. Kid or not, she was keeping the money, and there was nothing her mother could say to change her mind.

"Momma, I told you I don't know where any money is. I wish I did, but I don't." She tried to look miserable. "I know this is very sad, Momma, but we'll be okay."

The pleading left her mother's face, replaced by the more familiar rage. "You just don't get it, do you? Your worthless father is dead. I have no money. Think, Dottie. Where is that money? You have to know. For God's sake child, why won't you tell me where it is?"

Dottie walked closer to the site, took a few of the stones that had been loosened from the ground, and placed them near the grave to mark its location. She stood there for a few minutes while her mother continued to rant, but she had long experience in ignoring her words. Instead, she looked around to make sure she could remember the site. When she turned and began walking, she walked past Momma, opened the car door, climbed in the back seat, and waited.

Finally exhausting all the foul language she knew, Cecilia returned to the car, go into it and put her head on the steering wheel for a while. When she sat back up, she looked at Dottie. "Well I guess we'll just have to go live in Detroit where I've got family. I hate Detroit, and you'll hate Detroit. But we have no choice."

Dottie knew she had to hide the money before their journey to Detroit. "When would we have to leave, Momma?"

"As soon as I can pack us up." Cecilia took a deep, shuddering breath. "I hope your sorry daddy left enough money to get us to Detroit. We'll be living with my aunt now."

Dottie was too afraid to ask what that last statement meant. And she'd never heard of Detroit. The answer didn't matter anyway. Right now, she was focused on hiding the money.

Cecilia dropped Dottie off at the house to go in search of a bar that was open at this hour. Dottie knew she'd be gone for a long time. That was okay. More time to think.

Chapter 36

 Washington, DC, 1934

Hirsh hung up the phone, left his office, walked downstairs, and saw Billy standing by the bar.

"Have you seen Edward?"

"He was just here. I told him you were upstairs and he headed that way. Didn't you see him?"

Hirsh thought about the phone conversation. Surely Edward hadn't heard him talking.

"Son, would you run to Tally's? We need some mixers for tonight."

"What do you want—"

"Doesn't matter. Just grab some tonic, and ginger ale."

"Yes sir." Hirsh sounded irritated, but Billy couldn't figure out why.

Hirsh watched Billy leave the club and went behind the bar for the cashbox, sliding out each brick with care. He grabbed the box out and knew right away the money was gone. He didn't have the heart to open it. He placed the box on the bar and stared at it. Edward. It had to be him. He'd been double-crossed by Edward. He'd always known that Edward was a no-good. He was nothing when he met him and he was less than nothing now. He'd have to think of a plan to explain the loss of money to his partner. Senator Hughes would never understand.

* * *

As soon as Dottie watched her mother drive away, she grabbed the tackle box and walked outside. She wrapped the box in a laundry bag and headed out the door. It was a long walk to the cemetery. She took her red wagon from the garage and loaded the box, adding a shovel. The shovel handle stuck out the back of the wagon, but otherwise it simply looked as though she was taking laundry to the neighborhood laundromat.

As she approached the cemetery, she slowed her steps and looked around. She didn't see anyone, but the clouds above her were getting dark and thick. Already it was harder to see the pine tree. More snow was coming, and she didn't want to get caught in it.

When she located the rocks she'd placed at the grave, she walked three child-sized paces to the left, and began to dig. When she thought the hole was deep enough, she placed rocks on the bottom. The box inside the laundry bag would be next, but she made no move to place it there, not yet. After thinking a moment, she looked around, and opened the top of the laundry bag, then the tackle box. From it she drew five one-hundred-dollar bills, and put them in her underwear, fearing her mother would check her coat pockets.

She closed the tackle box, pulled the laundry bag's drawstring tight, then carefully placed the bag with the tackle box and money inside on top of the rocks, and covered the box entirely with smaller rocks. Once satisfied that the rocks would provide enough shelter for the bag even if she was gone for a long time, she covered the rocks with a good amount of dirt and patted it down. She covered the area with a few sticks and brown leaves.

She didn't mark this hole's location; she knew where her dad was buried, and that her secret was right next to it.

Chapter 37

 Washington, DC, 2015

"I had to wait for my mother to die. I didn't want her to have any of the money. She was a disgrace, you see. I heard the fight, and knew that the money was your uncle's, not my father's." Dorothy looked at Clarence. "But I didn't know where your uncle went, and I didn't care. I just didn't want Momma to get any of the money. So I buried it next to Daddy."

Dorothy fixed me with a hard stare that I suspected was to cover hurt. Her account wasn't making much sense, yet there was an opening with her pause, so I took it.

"Let me see if I can fill in some spots here. Who killed your father?"

"Edward did. But it was an accident. My daddy found some money at the club, and Edward confronted him.

Daddy pulled out a gun, and in the fight over it, Edward accidently shot him. After he killed my daddy, he looked for the money in our house, but never found it."

"How much money?"

"A little over a hundred and eighty-five thousand dollars."

"That's a fair amount of money. Is any of it—"

Dorothy took a deep breath. "There's a lot more."

"I'm sorry ... what?" Clarence's face held surprise.

"There's a lot more," Dorothy repeated.

We all sat quiet for a moment until I said, "Care to explain?"

"I took five hundred dollars of that money with me. Mom and I moved back to Detroit. Then we moved to Atlanta. Then we moved to ... so many other places. Mom took to being a prostitute to make ends meet." Dorothy's chuckle was bitter. "I'm fairly sure she liked the work. With Roosevelt's New Deal, she had other choices, though I imagine none of those would have allowed her to drink. At least she never made me do that. I guess I ought to be grateful.

"When I was nineteen, we wound up back near Washington, DC. I hated my mother but she was all I had. It was too late to explain the money to her. Honestly I wouldn't have put it past her to get rid of me." Dorothy said this with a resolved calmness. I looked at her and didn't know what to say. We all sat in silence, and she continued.

"One afternoon while she was busy with a gentleman caller, I snuck out, took the bus to the cemetery, and I dug up the money with my hands. I didn't know what to do with it, so I got back on the bus with the bag. I wound up at the bus station. I took the bag with me inside the station and bought a locker. I left the money there for a while, so I could think of what to do next."

We were all staring at her in disbelief when Hank returned, carrying a cardboard carton from which wonderful scents emanated.

"Would you like to have something to eat before you continue?" I said.

She shook her head. "But you go on. Now that I've started talking, I might as well tell all of it."

Hank spread out the food on the room's table, and while we began eating, she began again.

"I knew I couldn't leave the money in a locker forever, and I was afraid to take it back to the cemetery. I didn't know if I could keep the weather from it. I couldn't take it to Momma's house. It was more of a one-room shanty, and I was afraid she'd find it.

"I was a kid with little schooling and no one to turn to. On the bus, I saw an ad about converting money to gold. I wrote down the phone number in that book you found in my room. It cost me $53.80 per ounce. That $185,000 bought me roughly 3,200 ounces. It turned out to be about eight bars. I had to give the dealer ten thousand."

Costly transaction, I thought, but not important right now. "Gold is worth about $1,200 per ounce today." I whipped out my phone and opened the calculator app. "Why that's about—"

Dorothy chimed in proudly "About four million dollars. And that much gold was heavy."

Clarence asked, astonished, "You have almost four million in gold?"

"Well, not exactly."

"Not exactly? How much is left, and where is it now?"

"I didn't know what to do with it. After all it was stolen money to begin with. I was nineteen years old, and a woman besides." Dorothy took a long breath.

"I don't know how her liver lasted as long as it did, but Momma died when I was fifty or so. Of course she was penniless, and I was a simple cashier with no money. When she'd been gone about ten years, I decided to cash in some of the money to find a better place to live. I found a nice young attorney who listened to my story. He said not to worry about the money being stolen as it had happened so long ago, I had more than enough money to take care of me until I die. He's the one who told me about Fountain View."

She sighed deeply again, a noise so unexpected from her we all stopped eating. "Are you all right?" I said, wondering if the sleeping pills were still affecting her.

"Oh, I'm fine. I just always have trouble with remembering the what-happened-next. You see, I thought I was set for the rest of my life, and I could stop worrying. Then one of the fellows at Fountain View learned about the gold and found out about the Mayflower Club, just like you did."

I put my plastic fork down. "Is that why they guarded you so carefully at Fountain View?"

"No, not really. My attorney set it up that as long as I didn't die suspiciously, the home would be the beneficiaries of the gold."

I nodded. "And where is all this gold?"

"The cemetery's around here somewhere—"

"Whispering Pines?" Clarence and I asked as one.

Dorothy's face showed surprise. "How did you know?"

"We found a paper in an old tin box with the name of the cemetery on it," I said.

Clarence's gaze remained on Dorothy. "You mean you buried the gold in that cemetery all those years ago?"

"Well, where else would I put it?" As if the question wasn't a logical one.

"Is it still there?" Clarence asked, obviously riveted by her story.

"It should be. Buried next to my daddy," Dorothy nonchalantly replied. "But not as much as it started. I had to convert one of the gold bars to pay the attorney, and Fountain View. What's left is at Whispering Pines. I figured no one would find it there. There must be about three and a half million left."

We were all astonished. No one spoke for a moment. When I found my voice I said, "Would you ... be willing to take us there?"

"Well, here's the thing ..." At Dorothy's pause, we all stared at her.

"Like I said a minute ago, it's stated in my will that Fountain View gets the gold. I don't have any relatives, and they know they'll get it after my death."

I decided it was time to lay out the complete story, the part Dorothy couldn't possibly know. "Dorothy ... there's been a guy following us around. Starting with Clarence. His name is Jim, we think. We broke into his house, and found a key to the cashbox where Edward had stored the cash at the club, *and* an invoice from Fountain View for his services. He's been intimidating everyone. Seems to me he was working for Fountain View, in an effort to find the gold."

"Blond-hair guy with some sort of drawing on his neck?" I nodded, and she replied, "I was suspicious of him too. He was asking me all sorts of questions, like I was some dimwitted old person that might spill the beans." She giggled. "I believe he worked for them, or at least he did at first. When he realized how much money I had, I think he planned to take it and skip town. Think about it ... unless he told them, Fountain View had no idea how much money was at stake ..." Her eyes turned sad. "Or maybe he was hired by them—to find out how much money I had *and* how eager they ought to be to see me gone."

I considered this. "Dorothy, he *was* hired by Fountain View. The invoice confirms it. Edward lived for years believing the money was out there somewhere. No one believed *him* until Clarence found evidence to the contrary. Then he hired me, and for a while, I was the only one who believed him. Does Clarence want any part of the money? Sure he does. But he also wants to prove that his uncle wasn't lying—"

Clarence finally spoke up. "Listen Dorothy, Uncle Edward didn't plan on stealing that money from the club. He thought that he and your granddaddy were partners. That they'd split the money someday. Something happened between him and Hirsh Rosenburg, but he would never talk about it."

That sat for a minute. Until Dorothy stood up. "Let's take a ride."

We piled into Clarence's car. The drive to Whispering Pines was a quiet one. We all had questions, but knew that Dorothy had to process all this. Pushing her didn't seem prudent. Or fair, considering all the mysteries she'd helped us clear up.

We arrived at the cemetery. Dorothy looked around and started to walk, but the terrain was noticeably unstable. She stumbled slightly on a small patch of weeds. Clarence and Hank each took an arm and we made our way through the cemetery toward the old pine tree.

It was at this point I began to wonder if bringing Hank was a good move. We were all caught up in the moment. I'd never considered his criminal past might be a problem. But who wouldn't be tempted at a winner-take-all outcome, "all" meaning the gold?

Hank carried a gun. I was carrying a hotel key. I began to survey the area. There were branches and rocks lying around. Not much defense against a handgun. If Hank's intentions weren't honorable, best case, we'd take bars of gold with us. Worst case, we'd be buried in an old cemetery. I couldn't recruit two old people's help. This was up to me. And since dying wasn't on today's agenda, I continued glancing around for any type of weapon.

We approached the pine tree, and Dorothy headed to a small grouping of rocks. She took three short steps and stopped, then pointed down, and as she looked at Clarence, I saw Hank whip out his gun. In that second I spotted a nice-sized rock and then heard "Duck now!"

While I was bent down to retrieve the rock, I heard a shot. I wasn't hit. I looked up. Clarence and Dorothy seemed to be okay too. I turned in the direction Hank was pointing his gun, and there, dropping to the ground, was a blond-haired man pointing a gun. At me. Before I had time enough to draw what I was certain would be my last breath, I heard a second shot.

"That should take care of him," I heard Hank say.

Dorothy stood tall, never wavering even as bullets were flying. I made it to a full standing position, somewhat shaken, and heard Clarence say, "Thanks, son."

Son? "You're ..."

"Yes Miss Mel, Hank's my son."

I couldn't respond. I'd just witnessed a shooting. There was a presumably dead man only a few feet away. Dorothy was about to uncover millions in gold ... and Clarence had a son named Hank. The last revelation wasn't that stunning, but regardless, there was a lot to process here.

Clarence look at Hank, a question in his eyes, and Hank replied with a nod and an offhand shrug. Then the old man's eyes returned to me.

"Hank made some questionable decisions in the past," he explained. "Spent a little time in jail. He's straightened his life out. I hated bringing him in on this, but he insisted. I had to promise I wouldn't talk about his past, so I just never said anything."

Hank. Clarence's son. Once my mind stopped reeling, I recalled how close they'd seemed to be. How concerned Clarence was for Hank after we broke into Jim-the-stalker's house. I'd missed it. Completely. Not much of a detective.

"You know Clarence, I would've been okay with it. Why didn't you tell me?"

"Just didn't seem that important."

In truth, he was right; it really didn't make a difference. I wanted to be upset but I let it go.

"I got a shovel in the trunk." Hank started walking toward the car.

"I declare, you all are a piece of work," Dorothy stated.

There was a small bench not far away. I pointed to it, she nodded, and I walked with her to the bench and sat there with her while Hank dug for the gold.

I looked at her. "I have to ask. So many years it was here. It could have been discovered by someone else. Why didn't you retrieve it?"

"The money meant nothing to me, Melinda. I had a mother who was a drunk and a prostitute. My daddy did things to me that I'd rather not recall." There were sudden tears in her eyes. "I was nine years old when I watched him die at Edward's hand. I knew Edward shot him in self-defense, but even that didn't matter."

We sat there for a moment, quiet, but then I had to tell her. "You know, Dorothy, we dredged up a past you obviously wanted to forget. For that, I am sorry. But it's just that, the past. You weren't happy being locked up at Fountain View. There are better places. With the money, you can live where you want to live. Please don't think you have to go back to Fountain View."

"That's *obviously* not possible now. I understand that."

I put my arm around Dorothy. "I can't tell you what to do but let me see this through. I have some suggestions but ... for right now, let's all just get through this day."

I stood and walked toward Clarence.

"How is she?" Clarence asked.

"Dorothy lived a disastrous childhood. One that we can't fix. One that money will never fix. We'll talk later."

"I called the police," Clarence said. "They should be here any minute. I have a feeling we'll be here for a while explaining all of this. Do you think they'll believe us?"

I didn't have an answer for that. I didn't have an answer for Dorothy. I didn't know what to do next. I sat down on the ground and leaned against the old pine tree, and heard the wailing of sirens as they approached the cemetery.

Epilogues

Hirsh Rosenburg

Hirsh never knew what happened to the money stashed in the cashbox, but learned who was responsible for it going missing. His daughter, Cecilia, also told him that George was killed by Edward. Through crocodile tears, she told him they were arguing over money. He knew her tears over George were phony, but he gave her a few hundred dollars for Dottie's sake. He knew she'd be back for more.

Not long after Cecilia's visit, the club was raided again. This time they found the gambling operation, which earned Hirsh a twelve-year prison sentence. Hirsh was convinced that Senator Hughes was behind the raid. The senator never understood the story about the missing money. For the rest of his life, Hirsh mourned the Mayflower Club, the club of his dreams. He was fairly certain that Edward had heard his phone call with the senator and that they'd planned his death.

Hirsh died of tuberculosis in prison. To the day he died, he wished he could tell Edward that he was sorry, that his choice of the Mayflower Club over their partnership was, in the end, a most regrettable decision. He never got that wish granted.

Edward Higgins

The very same day Edward heard Hirsh plotting his demise on the phone, he moved back to Detroit. He and Hirsh never spoke again. He spent a lifetime talking about the money to his relatives. His financial circumstances never permitted his returning to Washington, DC, to try and find its whereabouts. Ultimately, he had no idea where to look. Sadly, no one ever believed his story. But more devastating to Edward was that Hirsh, the only person he was ever close to, had planned to kill him over the money. He never trusted a single soul again. Edward died in 1972, still claiming there was money out there somewhere, a lot of it, and imploring his nephew Clarence to keep looking. "Find Dorothy Clemmons," Edward often told him. "She knows somethin'."

Billy Wade

Billy went on to a successful art career, and by the time of the post-raid public auction of the Mayflower Club's holdings, he was doing well enough to win the bid on the club's infamous mirror. When he died the mirror tiles had cracked in several places, but it was passed down to friends until it was recreated by an unknown artist and can today be viewed in its original location, DC.'s old Mayflower Club— or as it's known today, Dirty Martini.

Mel, et al

And what about Mel? Did she stay with Jaimie? And Clarence? Was he happy after he found the money?

Well, most days, when not in LA, you can find Melinda and Jaimie on the beach in Perth, Australia. After some deliberation Mel took that finder's fee, which helped save her business and made it possible to take time away with Jaimie, whenever she could.

And Dorothy? Through her attorney, Dorothy paid Fountain View the money she owed them, not a penny more, and removed them as her beneficiaries. Clarence and Dorothy converted the rest of the gold and split the money. Clarence sold the house in Detroit and bought a brownstone outside Washington, DC. Hank moved to Washington too, and dropped by when he wasn't otherwise occupied, but Clarence got lonely sometimes, and felt responsible for Dorothy. He asked her to live with him in the brownstone and she was plenty pleased to accept.

You might have called theirs a companionate love; they took walks around their neighborhood and dined at extravagant restaurants, and, each having lost so much and then gained parts back, they grew to care about each other. Dorothy passed away in her sleep in 2017. Months before she died, she thanked Clarence for at long last helping her find a most pleasant life. When she closed her eyes for that last time in her eighty-eighth year, she did so with a peaceful soul.

Epilogue II

"Hello? Is this Melinda Danbury?" I heard a gruff sounding voice asked as I answered my phone.

"Yes, this is Melinda. How can I help you? ... On Route 66, you say? ... You're looking for what? ... Well, I'm more of an archeologist— Say that again? ... I'll be back in LA in about two weeks. Call my office and let's meet to discuss."

"Who was that?" Jaimie asked when I clicked off.

Mel smiled. "You really don't want to know."

With raised eyebrows, he said, "I probably don't. Unless it will make a good movie."

Made in the USA
Las Vegas, NV
27 February 2023

68194308R00173